t . h . e

ACHIEVEMENT

p . a . r . a . d . o . x

t.h.e
ACHIEVEMENT
p.a.r.a.d.o.x

Test Your Personality &
Choose Your Behavior
for Success at Work

RONALD A. WARREN, PH.D.

NEW WORLD LIBRARY
NOVATO, CALIFORNIA

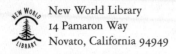

New World Library
14 Pamaron Way
Novato, California 94949

Edited by Georgia Hughes and Katharine Farnam Conolly
Front cover design by Mary Beth Salmon
Text design by Mary Ann Casler
Typography by Tona Pearce Myers

Grateful acknowledgment is given to Mark Brenner, Ph.D. at The Global
Consulting Partnership, for permission to use his Constructive Problem
Solving Model in chapter 6.

The material in this book is intended for education. No expressed or implied
guarantee as to the effects of the use of the recommendations can be given
nor liability taken.

Library of Congress Cataloging-in-Publication Data

Warren, Ronald Alan,
  The achievement paradox : test your personality & choose your behavior for
success at work /
By Ronald A. Warren.
      p.   cm.
Includes bibliographical references and index.
  ISBN 1-57731-228-7 (pbk. : alk. paper)
  1. Job satisfaction. 2. Achievement motivation. 3. Personality
assessment. 4. Personality tests. 5. Employees—Attitudes Evaluation. I,
Title.
  HF5549.5.J63 W37 2002
  650.1′3—dc21   2002007480

First Printing, October 2002
ISBN 1-57731-228-7
Printed in Canada on acid-free, partially recycled paper
Distributed to the trade by Publishers Group West

10   9   8   7   6   5   4   3   2   1

To my children,
Kelly and Will

c . o . n . t . e . n . t . s

i.n.t.r.o.d.u.c.t.i.o.n

W hat is the impact of personality style on job success and satisfaction? The latest studies show that personality plays an immense role in achievement. In the information-age workplace, intelligence, education, and technical skills are necessary but not sufficient for high performance on the job because personality, operating like a lens, either focuses or blurs all your other job-related skills and abilities. For twenty years I have developed personality assessments that are used by Fortune 1000 organizations to help managers understand their personality style as it relates to success and satisfaction in the workplace. Like many other psychologists, what I've found is that personality is not merely an important factor but can actually make or break you in on-the-job performance.

The Achievement Paradox is about your personality and its impact on your behavior, success, and satisfaction at work. Although personality has an immense impact upon how you feel, act, and react at work, people rarely take the time to understand how their personality style influences their work experiences. Studies and everyday experience show that personality can propel a person of fairly average intelligence and education to great heights or can make the smartest person feel like a failure. Personality colors everything.

Not only does your personality influence your experience at work but, for better or worse, so do the personalities of your work associates. If you are like most people, you spend more of your waking hours at work and with coworkers, vendors, and clients than you do with your family and friends. As many people I've worked with have said to me, lots of people in the work world "could use a personality adjustment." The interplay between your personality and the personality styles of your work associates is often intense, emotional, and can be a major source of stress.

Many people recognize the effect that a coworker's personality has on their productivity and job satisfaction but find it difficult to reflect objectively on their own personality and its impact on their work experiences. It is easier for people to blame their lack of success or feelings of discontentment on others, rather than to take a good, hard look at their own personality to assess where they get in the way of job success and satisfaction. And casual efforts to evaluate our own personality can lead to deceptive results.

David Meyers conducted a study in which professionals rated their own social and leadership skills.[1] One hundred percent of the respondents claimed that they were in the top half in social skills. One in four respondents placed themselves in the top 1 percent in social skills. Only one in fifty said they were in the bottom 25 percent in leadership capability. I describe this phenomenon as the Lake Wobegon effect, recalling Garrison Keillor's phrase, "where all the men are strong, all the women are pretty, and all the children are above average." In a study that I conducted, I discovered that 98 percent of people rate themselves as cooperative most of the time, yet when asked to rate the behavior of other people, only 35 percent were described as cooperative. This is the classic pattern of social desirability: people tend to describe their behavior as they think it should be rather than how it actually is.

To provide you with a strong foundation of knowledge about your personality style, in chapter 2 you will complete a reliable and validated assessment of your personality using the ACT Profile (ACT: Assessment of Character Traits). When you complete the ACT Profile on-line, you will receive a graphic display of your results — your ACT Self-Profile. Your self-assessment results serve as a personal benchmark to compare with research profiles of both highly effective and less-effective professionals. You will see in these research profiles that there are five success traits that are consistently associated with high performance across professions, and that there are five common personality traits that undermine performance and satisfaction on the job.

Current research shows that a majority of professionals rely on their intelligence, education, and job skills in their efforts to succeed yet spend little time trying to master personality traits that interfere with their attaining a higher level of performance. Most people have tremendous potential to dramatically increase their job success and satisfaction by

1. understanding their personality and its impact on their effectiveness,
2. appreciating that their personality is a critical asset that needs ongoing care and nurturing, and
3. taking greater responsibility to actively manage their personality at work.

This book is for people who want to understand their personality and learn how to consciously manage their behavior in order to find greater success and satisfaction in the workplace.

This sounds relatively straightforward, perhaps easy. But if it were easy, everyone would do it; and if you look around you, you will see that this is not the case.

People have built up psychological defenses and are afraid to take a good, hard look at their personality traits and behavior and to confront their shortcomings and deficits. Many people are uncomfortable examining their imperfections and would rather ignore their deficits than deal with them. Admitting to shortcomings is difficult and takes courage. We live in a society where people do not want to appear vulnerable or show weakness. Yet, when individuals do reveal their vulnerabilities, others often rally to support them.

Acknowledging the need to change your behavior to become more effective is not an indictment of your character but a sign of character strength. Confronting your shortcomings not only is the best way to overcome them but also allows you to better capitalize on your strengths. Understanding your personality opens up opportunities to make well-informed decisions about how to better manage your behavior to achieve what you want to achieve. That is what this book is all about.

The goal of this book is to help you recognize and understand which of your personality traits are assets and which get in your way, and to develop the skills necessary to consciously direct your behavior toward greater success and satisfaction at work.

This book is designed to parallel the processes and methods that have been successfully used in my work in corporate seminars and workshops (for more information, visit achievementparadox.com). As in the seminars, in this book you will assess your personality, examine the research on effective and ineffective personality traits, and combine the information to make informed decisions on the kinds of behaviors you can develop to be more successful and satisfied at work.

Most important, the key common denominator in this book and in the seminars is *you*. Only you can make the effort to learn about the person you are and then decide what kind of person you would like to be. Only you can make the commitment and effort to move beyond just thinking about your personality strengths and weaknesses and work to change your behavior. Change does not miraculously occur simply by attending a seminar or by reading a book; it occurs when you supply the attention, courage, and energy to continue the day-to-day work involved in behavioral change and self-development.

Note

1.   See the citation of *The Inflated Self,* by David Myers, in "How Do I Love Me? Let Me Count the Ways," *Psychology Today* (May 1980): 16.

c . h . a . p . t . e . r   1

PERSONALITY AND HUMAN CAPITAL

A re you ready to accept a challenge, a challenge that
will improve your work life and offer benefits of success, no matter what type of work or profession you
pursue? This challenge relates to what I call the achievement
paradox — the paradox of why what got you your job might
not be what you need to keep your job and improve your
career.

The paradox of achievement in today's work world is
that organizations place a premium on intellect, education,
and technical knowledge — the "hard skills" that are the
cost of entry into the work world — but more often than
not, it is personality that determines who survives and
thrives on the job. IQ, education, technical knowledge,
and skills are necessary but not sufficient for success and
satisfaction in today's economy.

In this information age, where corporations refer to
people as knowledge workers and human capital, it is
tempting to think that your IQ, education, and technical

knowledge will determine your career success. However, because today's workforce is more intelligent, educated, and technically savvy than ever before, few people have a competitive advantage simply because of their hard skills.

You can find the competitive edge you are seeking by making a disciplined effort to learn about your personality and your behavior — the so-called "soft skills." With reliable information about which aspects of your personality are assets and which are liabilities, you can learn to change your behavior and to achieve your professional goals.

The assessment, research studies, and examples in this book will help you learn how to better manage your personality so that it is a key asset in your unique package of knowledge, skills, and abilities: your human capital. With some dedication and effort, you can make the most of the human in your human capital.

What Is Human Capital?

Human capital is today's hot term for the sum total of knowledge and skills that you bring to your work. Companies spend millions of dollars annually on research to define and measure the components of human capital most relevant to job performance and business success. Study results influence policies and procedures in the hiring, training, compensation, promotion, and termination of employees. Personality measures are the core of employee selection tests that organizations use to decide if a job candidate has what is needed for high performance. Personality more accurately predicts business success than knowledge or skills, because personality functions as the manager of all workplace abilities, and the best human resource managers know this. Personality is the element at the core of the work experience, and it has a huge impact on personal productivity and job satisfaction.

Human capital includes IQ, education, technical knowledge, job-specific skills, professional experience, work ethic, and personality. Each component in this equation contributes to your value in the marketplace, but there are significant differences between these components of human capital. Although many people believe that personality and behavior styles are unchangeable, compared to the other components of human capital, personality and behavior are in fact the most easily modified. Consider the following:

> ## Rate Yourself
>
> (1) Given your IQ, education, technical skills, and work ethic, does your personality work to optimize or diminish the value of these hard skills? (2) How does your personality impact the way in which you experience your work life? (3) Does your personality influence whether your current path to success is smooth and easy or rocky and difficult?

1. You can't increase your IQ because it peaks in your early twenties.
2. You cannot dramatically increase your creativity or common sense; these appear to be inborn and relatively set by adulthood.
3. You can increase your education, but not without huge investments of time and money.
4. You can develop your technical skills, but that requires time and is limited by IQ and opportunity.
5. You can gain more experience, but experience takes time and is a constant that operates equally for all.
6. You can increase your work hours in an attempt to increase your productivity, but this often leads to burnout and job dissatisfaction.

Compared to the obstacles to change presented by the other components of human capital, a self-directed effort to

What's a personality disorder? Everyone has personality traits and many people have personality traits that interfere with their achieving success and satisfaction. But simply interfering with high performance and personal satisfaction does not equate to a personality disorder. A personality disorder is a chronic pattern of feelings and behaviors that significantly deviate from the cultural expectations, resistant to change, and cause significant impairment. Conservative estimates are that 20 percent of people have a personality disorder.[1] What kinds of feelings and behaviors characterize a personality disorder? Here are a few examples: the dependent personality disorder passively allows others to assume responsibility for major areas of life... subordinates own needs... lacks self-confidence. The histrionic personality disorder shows an incessant drawing of attention to oneself ... is perceived by others as shallow and lacking genuineness... vain and demanding. The narcissistic personality disorder has a grandiose sense of self-importance... entitlement... interpersonal exploitativeness. I presented this symptom checklist to an audience and one of the people shouted out "Hey that's my team!"

understand your personality and to consciously modify your behavior is a fast, inexpensive track toward professional development. There are no time limitations, no special access to opportunity, no constraints except those you impose on yourself, and the only cost is the mental energy you expend in making a significant effort to think before you act. In fact, simply by making an effort to change some element of your behavior, you make progress. In the case of behavior change, often the means is the end.

What Is Personality?

Since this book is all about personality, you may be asking, What is personality? People tend to think of personality as purely internal: motivations, thoughts, and feelings, almost as if it were separate from behavior. Psychologists may not agree on one definition of personality, but there is strong agreement that personality includes how you act, the impression you create in others, and your typical patterns of behavior.[2]

In addition to agreement

that personality is not just an internal phenomenon but is expressed in your behavior, psychologists also agree that personality traits can either positively accentuate or compromise the skills and abilities you bring to the workplace. Recent studies show that personality and character are much stronger predictors of success than IQ or book smarts.[3] Organizational psychologists estimate that 75 percent of people in the workforce have personality traits that hinder job performance. This percentage may seem incredibly high, but, from my experience, it is accurate and is the reason Scott Adams does not lack material for his popular *Dilbert* cartoon.

Such counterproductive personality traits not only hinder one's own job performance but also, in others, are a huge source of stress in the workplace. Robert Hogan, chairman of the University of

The Ten Most Common Acts of Aggression in the Workplace

1. Talking about someone behind their back
2. Interrupting others while they are speaking or working
3. Flaunting status or authority; acting in a condescending manner
4. Belittling someone's opinion to other workers
5. Failing to return phone calls or respond to memos
6. Giving others the silent treatment
7. Insulting, yelling, and shouting
8. Verbal forms of sexual harassment
9. Staring, dirty looks, or other negative eye contact
10. Using forms of praise to actually damn someone[4]

Oklahoma organizational psychology department, notes counterproductive personality traits as the leading cause of employee stress and discontent. He cites studies showing that "since the 1950s, 70 percent of employees surveyed have said that the worst, most stressful part of their job is their immediate boss." In another study, Harvey Hornstein, a psychology professor at Columbia University, surveyed a thousand people and found that 90 percent claimed that, at some point in their career, they had worked for a "brutal boss" who publicly humiliated them or blamed them for his own failures. Hornstein estimates that at least 20 percent of employees are under a manager who is a "brutal boss." His research is consistent with findings by David Campbell, a senior fellow at the Center for Creative Leadership, who says, "We've had managers come to our center who actually defined leadership as the ability to inflict pain."[5]

Now that you have an idea of what personality is and how important it is in determining your success and satisfaction at work, let's look at its role in getting and keeping a job.

The Central Role of Personality in Securing Employment

Personality is the key that unlocks the door to a new job in any type of employment — factory worker, salesperson, scientist, manager, or top executive. A U.S. Census Bureau study of three thousand employers revealed that attitude is the most important factor in a hiring decision. On a scale of 1 to 5, with 5 ranking as very important, attitude was at 4.6, followed by communication skills at 4.2, work experience at 4.0, and references at 3.4. A 2002 survey of Fortune 1000 company executives showed that leadership and management skills are the most sought after, with technology skills a distant third. The executives stated that currently one out of every three employees is unable to collaborate effectively with coworkers and that employment success in the future would increasingly depend on the ability to demonstrate the personality traits that allow for high levels of teamwork and cooperation in the workplace.

Corporations spend hundreds of millions of dollars each year on preemployment selection tests, and they invest this money because they know that the money spent is nominal compared to the cost of hiring and training an employee who doesn't work out. Personality flaws are often subtle and difficult to detect during interviews. Job applicants can create a very good impression during an interview by relying on their intelligence and their ability to be articulate and by turning on the charm to successfully disguise or diminish negative personality traits that will later prove troublesome. Even individuals who turn out to be disastrous employees and are later terminated are able to be on their best behavior for the few hours of a job interview. Organizations have tried to combat this by asking applicants to cite specific examples of desirable behaviors (sets high standards, teamwork, conscientiousness, flexibility). But it is difficult to confirm the validity of a job applicant's previous work behavior because former employers, fearing a lawsuit, will usually only verify dates of employment, and will steer clear of describing an ex-employee's personality.

The result is that many people who have undesirable personality traits end up being hired. They don't behave on the job as their successful interviews would lead others to expect and so contribute to creating very stressful workplaces.

The Importance of Your Personality in Keeping Your Job

When a major corporation decides to lay off forty thousand employees, how does it decide who will be pink-slipped?

In 1996 AT&T had to make this difficult choice. It decided to have managers rate their subordinates on leadership, teamwork, and communication skills and to use the assessment results as a part of the evaluation package that determined job cuts. This case represents one of the more extreme uses of a formalized assessment process for terminations that I have come across, but it demonstrates how well established the link is between personality and your ability to keep a job.

The Center for Creative Leadership (CCL) is a well-respected, nonprofit institute based in North Carolina that is dedicated to the study of management and executive leadership. Researchers at CCL coined the term "derailment" to describe how high-potential, fast-track managers are skipped over for promotions or are terminated because of personality flaws. Although the CCL studies focus on managers and executives in positions of leadership, their findings can be generalized to almost any type of employment. CCL lists twenty-six derailment traits, including difficulty handling pressure, interpersonal insensitivity, lack of team skills, arrogance, and relying too much on natural talents. Natural talents such as intelligence and technical talent may put you on the fast track to success, but at some point in your career, self-management and interpersonal skills become essential, and counterproductive personality traits are unacceptable.

A survey of 150 CEOs revealed that the most common reason for a senior executive to be terminated was a lack of insight into their behavior; 77 percent of the CEOs said "the newly departed were in desperate need of an impartial, no-holds-barred performance evaluation."[6] While there is a tremendous focus on the impact of personality on executive performance — perhaps because executives are notorious for developing big egos — personality has a huge impact on the ability of any employee to maintain and grow in their career.

CCL specializes in the study of executives, a group that has many advantages over people in nonexecutive positions, including higher pay, more stock options, or vacation time, and the benefit of professional help when their personality styles are causing problems at work. It is commonplace for organizations to use assessments to help executives understand their personality strengths and weaknesses and to develop new behaviors where they have flaws. Many executives hire an executive coach to help in their self-development and/or attend training classes to avoid being blindsided by a job termination. Despite the help available, many executives believe that their other talents excuse their behavior flaws. They discount the important influence of their personality on their employment security and end up derailed in their careers, never knowing what hit them. The lessons learned through studies of executives are applicable to any employee — because whether you are an executive or work the swing shift, your personality can make or break you on the job.

Habits and Behavior Change

Most behavior patterns, effective or ineffective, result from habits and spontaneous reactions to situations, and not from self-conscious, self-directed efforts. For most of us, the gap between habitual responses and thoughtful responses is huge. Making a small change in the way we act can yield significant gains. For example, consider an overaggressive, impatient manager who is also a poor listener. This type of person tends to interrupt others, degrade communications, and is viewed as difficult and rude. Yet, through an awareness of their predisposition to interrupt and a conscious effort to monitor the

Behavioral feedback is valuable for not only at-risk individuals who want to retain their job but also organizations: companies that provide behavioral feedback have a better chance of retaining valued employees. A survey of employees by Personnel Decisions Inc. found that 80 percent of the respondents said that receiving feedback, an individual development plan, and nontechnical-skills training would make them less likely to seek employment elsewhere. However, only one in four respondents had an individual development plan, and only four of ten companies had programs to help these workers develop their nontechnical skills. More than 80 percent of respondents said they'd be more likely to stay with a company that offered comprehensive feedback on performance, but only 12.5 percent were currently receiving it.[7]

habit, such an individual can learn to suppress this negative behavior. By changing one behavior, an otherwise aggressive, impatient person can dramatically reduce the number of times that they irritate others and increase the opportunities to hear their coworkers' insights regarding work-related matters. (By the way, conservative estimates indicate that one in four people can be considered overaggressive, impatient, and poor listeners.)

Most of our behavior patterns are driven strictly by habit, what I call "default behaviors," that are not consciously directed. Many people think that personality and behavior are "hardwired" and thus cannot be changed. But this is not true. While a considerable effort is required to break longtime patterns, it does not require that you undergo dramatic personality changes. When you become more conscious of how your personality affects yourself and others, you take a giant step toward modifying your behavior. Much as a conductor uses a baton to quiet the horn section and bring up the strings, you can learn to consciously orchestrate your behavior.

Assessing Your Personality Traits

Of course, before you can make wise decisions and begin changing the behaviors that interfere with achievement and satisfaction in your work life, you need to know what those behaviors are. In the next chapter you will complete the ACT Profile to assess your personality traits. The resulting ACT Self-Profile will not only become your benchmark for understanding your current behavior but also provide you with a sense of what direction you will need to go in to build new, more effective behavior styles that fit your specific needs and wants. This test is based on statistical research I have done over the past twenty years with a wide range of professionals. (This work is discussed in detail in chapter 4.) Over one million professionals, in organizations including United

Parcel Service, Walt Disney World Attractions, Continental Insurance, Prudential Insurance, Silicon Graphics, Gannett Publishing, Virginia Power and Light, Consumers Union, Citibank, Rockwell International, and British Airways, have used personality assessments that I have developed. These assessments help employees to learn new behavior skills that are essential for effectiveness in leadership, teamwork, communications, project work, and conflict management.

Developing Your Powers of Self-Observation

The ACT Profile will help you to understand how your personality predisposes you to behave in a particular manner and to understand which behaviors are effective and which get in the way. From there, you can then develop your ability to consciously monitor and direct your behavior. Psychologists call the ability to monitor our own attitudes, feelings, and thoughts as having an "observing ego." The observing ego is a healthy expression of the ego that operates as the general manager of your be-

> A successful professional goes to a psychiatrist complaining of "feeling paranoid that other people think I'm an ass." The psychiatrist and client talk for forty-five minutes. The psychiatrist draws the session to a close by saying, "I have good news and bad news. The good news is that you don't have a paranoid personality disorder; the bad news is you are an ass."

havior. The job of the ego is to organize your mental processes so that you can function effectively in the world. (Note that this use of the word *ego* is altogether different from the colloquial use of the word, as in the phrase "he has a big ego.") When you develop your observing ego, you are self-aware, can think before you act, and can consciously make sure to express constructive rather than destructive behaviors.

This ability to consciously guide your behavior in order to raise your level of competence is popularized in a psychological model called "conscious competence." A person with conscious competence is one with a well-developed observing ego, who consciously guides his or her expression of constructive behaviors that are productive (rather than destructive behaviors, which are counterproductive). In addition to conscious competence, the three other psychological states of awareness in this model are unconscious competence, conscious incompetence, and unconscious incompetence.

- Unconscious competence: competence and skills that come naturally to you without your needing to make a conscious effort. People who are unconsciously competent are relatively rare, estimated at approximately 20 percent of the population, and truly have a special talent. These are folks who naturally "have their act together."

- Conscious incompetence: incompetence that you are aware of yet make no effort to correct or improve. Sometimes these consciously incompetent people are intelligent and talented professionals who are technically skilled. Because they are skilled, they expect their inappropriate behavior to be excused by others; they assume they will be excused because they are "key contributors." "Prima donna" is a term frequently applied to these people.

- Unconscious incompetence: incompetence that an individual is truly oblivious to. Unconsciously incompetent people have "blind spots." For example, consider a person like Frank, who describes himself as friendly, warmhearted, and empathetic. Yet Frank acknowledges that he is pushy, impatient with others, loses his temper, and angers easily. Most people experience Frank as pushy, impatient, and angry; they do not perceive him as friendly, warm, and empathetic. Nonetheless, Frank truly believes he is socially skilled — despite the fact that he acknowledges behaving in ways

that are not sociable. Frank is unconsciously incompetent in the area of social skills.

Few people are unconsciously competent, some are consciously competent, and most people are consciously or unconsciously incompetent. Most people have a personality
style that could use some fine-
tuning. Some of these people
are conscious of their need to
develop new behavioral skills
and some are not.

David Dunning, a psychology
professor at Cornell University, has added new information to the concept of
unconscious incompetence.
His studies have found that
people who are unconsciously
incompetent grossly overestimate their skills in areas
where they are deficient, to
such a great extent that they
are more confident of their
skills than people who have
actually mastered the skill.
Dunning explains that this
gap reflects a "deficiency in
self-monitoring skills," or a
lack of observing-ego skills.

Many people are defensive
regarding their shortcomings
and would rather not confront
personal development needs.
Some people find comfort in
the fact that 75 percent of
people have personality flaws
— so imperfection is the norm.
But this state of psychological
disrepair doesn't have to be the
end of the story. Key lessons
can be learned from individuals who have truly outstanding
self-management and interpersonal skills and business savvy.
These skills can be developed, and this book is a guide to
their development.

The Next Step

The next step in your development is to complete the ACT
Profile assessment. In the following chapter you will have
the option of completing your self-assessment on-line, as
recommended, or by filling out the assessment forms in the
chapter. After completing your assessment, you will have a
better sense of your strengths, weaknesses, and development

agenda. You can then proceed through the book using your ACT Self-Profile as a personal benchmark to compare to the research studies, to reflect on the case studies and examples, and, ultimately, to craft an action plan tied specifically to your development needs and wants.

Notes

1. American Psychiatric Association, *Diagnostic and Statistical Manual of Mental Disorders — DSM IV* (Washington: American Psychiatric Publishing, Inc., 1995).

2. Gardner Lindzey, et al., *Theories of Personality* (New York: John Wiley & Sons, 1997); Richard Arvey, *Fairness in Selecting Employees* (Reading, Mass.: Addison-Wesley Publishing. Co., 1988); and Raymond Cattell, *The Scientific Analysis of Personality* (San Diego, Calif.: Academic Press, 1977).

3. Daniel Goleman, *Emotional Intelligence* (New York: Bantam Books, 1995); Robert Kelley and Janet Caplan, "How Bell Labs Creates Star Performers," *Harvard Business Review* 71 (July–August 1993): 128–139; Robert Sternberg, *Successful Intelligence* (New York: Penguin Books, 1997); and Victor Dulewicz and Peter Herbert, "Predicting Advancement to Senior Management from Competencies and Personality Data: A Seven-Year Follow-Up Study," *British Academy of Management* 10 (1999): 13–22.

4. Harvey Hornstein, "Getting Bullied at Work," *San Francisco Chronicle* (19 October, 1998): E3.

5. David Campbell, "The College Say Exec Charisma Not All That Charming," *Chicago Tribune* 128 (1990); Robert Hogan, "Incompetent Managers Cause Stress," *Training Magazine* (August 1991): 10; Harvey Hornstein, "Getting Bullied at Work," *San Francisco Chronicle* (19 October, 1998): E3.

6. Manchester Partners, "Hey, Hot Shot, Take a Good Look at Yourself," *Fortune* (11 November, 1996): 211–212.

7. Carla Joinson, "Employee, Sculp Thyself...With a Little Help." *HR Magazine* 46, No. 5 (May 2001): 61–64.

c . h . a . p . t . e . r 2

THE ASSESSMENT OF CHARACTER TRAITS (ACT)

The Assessment of Character Traits (ACT) Profile presented in this chapter is designed to evaluate personality traits that have the greatest impact on work behavior. The ACT builds upon nearly four decades of published research. The ACT Profile that you complete will serve as your reference point to personalize all the information in the chapters that follow.

The personality information gleaned from taking this assessment will assist you in making more conscious and well-informed choices on how to work more effectively in the future. Of course, everyone has a blend of strengths and weaknesses, and there are no right or wrong answers, just more or less accurate answers that reflect who you are. Be honest and straightforward in answering the questions; keep an open mind, and remember that this information is intended solely for your personal development.

Completing the ACT Online

If you have access to the Internet, I strongly recommend that you complete your self-assessment online, at www.psychtests.com/act/. The online assessment provides four advantages over completing the assessment in the book.

1. The assessment items are generated in a random order, allowing for a more reliable and valid measure of your personality and character traits.
2. The online version instantaneously scores your ACT Self-Profile, which is much quicker than scoring your assessment on your own.
3. The online version generates your personal ACT Profile, which you can print and use for reference while reading the other chapters in this book.
4. For a small fee, the online version goes beyond providing an ACT Profile; it analyzes your overall ACT Profile results and provides a fifteen-page interpretation report.

So, if you have access to the Internet, go now to www.psychtests.com/act/ to complete your self-assessment and then return and begin reading the next chapter, "The ACT Profile Landmarks."

Completing the ACT Here

If you are unable to complete the assessment online, you can complete it in the following pages.

Your ACT Profile

To complete the following assessment, rate how well each of the following sixty-four words and phrases describe you. Rate yourself honestly, not how you would like to be (you will have the opportunity to assess how you would like to be in a later chapter). Don't fake being nice, or tough, or calm and collected because you think those are the appropriate characteristics. There are no right or wrong answers, just answers that reflect who you are. Remember that this information is intended solely for your personal development.

Rate yourself on each assessment item using the five-point scale below:

1 = Not at all like you

2

3 = Sometimes like you

4

5 = Like you to a great extent

1. _____ Trust others
2. _____ Patient
3. _____ Supportive and encouraging
4. _____ Available to others
5. _____ Have concern for others
6. _____ Cooperative

7. _____ Like meeting new people
8. _____ Develop positive relationships
9. _____ Gregarious and friendly
10. _____ Warmhearted
11. _____ More open than reserved
12. _____ Love to interact with others

13. _____ Want to please everyone
14. _____ Very concerned with what others think
15. _____ Work hard to be liked by others
16. _____ Need to be liked by others
17. _____ Want the approval of others
18. _____ Confrontational*

19. _____ Not assertive
20. _____ Prefer to follow
21. _____ Defer to others
22. _____ Submissive

23. _____ Independent*
24. _____ Have high standards*

25. _____ Tense and uneasy
26. _____ Apprehensive and unsure
27. _____ Insecure, lack self-confidence
28. _____ Calm and collected*

29. _____ Narrow-minded
30. _____ Do not listen
31. _____ Inflexible
32. _____ Stubborn
33. _____ Mistrustful
34. _____ Open-minded*

35. _____ Self-centered, egotistical
36. _____ Bossy, dictatorial
37. _____ Forceful, pushy
38. _____ Criticize others
39. _____ Controlling, dominating
40. _____ Express confidence in others*

41. _____ Work to outdo others
42. _____ Make everything a competition
43. _____ Measure success by wins
44. _____ Brag about winning
45. _____ Let everyone know who won and who lost
46. _____ Need to bury the competition

47. _____ Disciplined
48. _____ Detail oriented
49. _____ Careful, precise
50. _____ Do things right
51. _____ Do not plan ahead*
52. _____ Disorganized*

53. _____ Ambitious
54. _____ Like challenges
55. _____ Enjoy work
56. _____ Aspire to excel
57. _____ Like to learn
58. _____ Content with the status quo*

59. _____ Clever
60._____ Confident
61. _____ Generate new ideas
62._____ Imaginative, creative
63. _____ Inquisitive, curious about things
64._____ Prefer a low-risk approach*

Calculating the Correct Value for Each Assessment Item

The asterisk next to some of the assessment items denotes that those items must be reverse scored in order to obtain an accurate profile. Note that unless you reverse score the asterisked items (18, 23, 24, 28, 34, 40, 51, 52, 58, and 64) your ACT Profile will be inaccurate. Use the following table to convert your scores on these ten items:

- if you rated an item a 5, score it as a 1
- if you rated an item a 4, score it as a 2
- if you rated an item a 3, score it as a 3
- if you rated an item a 2, score it as a 4
- if you rated an item a 1, score it as a 5

With reverse scoring completed, calculate the total score for each group of assessment items; these groups are referred to as scales (Scale 1, Scale 2, et cetera) in the table below, and the items belonging to each group appear in the right column of the table. The item numbers in parentheses refer to those that require reverse scoring.

Total Scores

_____ Total Scale 1 = items 1 + 2 + 3 + 4 + 5 + 6

_____ Total Scale 2 = items 7 + 8 + 9 + 10 + 11 + 12

_____ Total Scale 3 = items 13 + 14 + 15 + 16 + 17 + (18)

_____ Total Scale 4 = items 19 + 20 + 21 + 22 + (23) + (24)

_____ Total Scale 5 = items 25 + 26 + 27 + (28)

_____ Total Scale 6 = items 29 + 30 + 31 + 32 + 33 + (34)

_____ Total Scale 7 = items 35 + 36 + 37 + 38 + 39 + (40)

_____ Total Scale 8 = items 41 + 42 + 43 + 44 + 45 + 46

_____ Total Scale 9 = items 47 + 48 + 49 + 50 + (51) + (52)

_____ Total Scale 10 = items 53 + 54 + 55 + 56 + 57 + (58)

_____ Total Scale 11 = items 59 + 60 + 61 + 62 + 63 + (64)

Plotting Your Scores on the ACT Profile

The ACT Profile you are about to plot shows your results in percentiles for each of the eleven ACT personality traits (each group of assessment items corresponds to a trait). Percentiles provide you with a comparison of your specific personality traits relative to other people. Raw scores do not provide this kind of comparison because some scales just naturally have lots of high scores and some scales do not. For instance, a raw score of 20 on Scale 2 (Sociable) converts to the twentieth percentile, while a raw score of 20 on Scale 7 (Controlling) converts to the ninety-seventh percentile.

In order to plot your ACT Profile on the blank profile below,

1. Go to the table below and find your raw score in the left column for each of the eleven scales and then circle the percentile score in the right column that corresponds to your raw score.

2. Make five copies of the blank profile ("Your ACT Self-Profile") on the following page so that you have several with which to work.

3. Take your eleven percentile scores and mark where each percentile score falls in the profile and then shade in the scale segment from the center point out to the mark you have made (an example of a scored and shaded profile appears at the end of this chapter).

The ACT Profile is made up of four concentric circles that correspond to the twenty-fifth, fiftieth, seventy-fifth, and hundredth percentiles, with the hundredth percentile forming the outermost edge of the profile. For example, if your raw score on Scale 1, Helpfulness, is 24, your percentile score is 44, which falls just below the fiftieth percentile circle. If your raw score on Scale 1 is 27, your percentile score is 82, which falls above the seventy-fifth percentile circle and below the hundredth percentile circle.

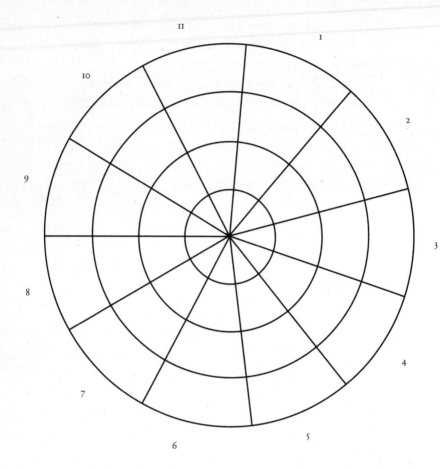

1. Helpfulness   5. Tense   9. Conscientious
2. Sociable   6. Rigid   10. Achieving
3. Need for Approval   7. Controlling   11. Innovative
4. Dependent   8. Competitive

The profile above is a picture, or map, of your personality. Your ACT Self-Profile shows which traits dominate your personality (the longest shadings) and those with the least influence on your personality (the shortest shadings). It is a snapshot of your personality traits as you perceived them when you completed the assessment. Although personality traits tend to be stable across time and place, your scores may change depending on your mood and current life events.

The ACT Profile you generated reflects how you see your-self. This may be closely related or very different from how others see you. (In chapter 5, you will complete an ACT Profile based on how you think others perceive you.) Chapter 3 provides a guide to learning about each of the eleven assessment scales and the key sectors within the ACT Profile.

Scale 1 Helpfulness		Scale 2 Sociable		Scale 3 Need for Approval	
Raw Score	Percentile	Raw Score	Percentile	Raw Score	Percentile
0–15	0	0–13	0	0–9	0
16	1	14	1	10	1
17	3	15	2	11	2
18	5	16	3	12	5
19	6	17	5	13	8
20	9	18	6	14	11
21	11	19	8	15	13
22	22	20	14	16	18
23	29	21	18	17	25
24	44	22	22	18	36
25	58	23	31	19	45
26	69	24	36	20	51
27	82	25	47	21	62
28	92	26	57	22	71
29	97	27	67	23	78
30	100	28	78	24	82
		29	88	25	89
		30	100	26	94
				27	97
				28	99
				29	100

Scale 4 Dependent		Scale 5 Tense		Scale 6 Rigid	
Raw Score	Percentile	Raw Score	Percentile	Raw Score	Percentile
0–5	0	0–3	0	0–5	0
6	7	4	6	6	7
7	13	5	18	7	11
8	20	6	37	8	19
9	32	7	54	9	28
10	45	8	68	10	44
11	53	9	71	11	53
12	62	10	84	12	67
13	68	11	91	13	77
14	76	12	96	14	84
15	82	13	98	15	89
16	87	14	100	16	94
17	92			17	96
18	94			18	97
19	96			19	98
20	98			20	100
21	100				

Scale 7 Controlling		Scale 8 Competitive		Scale 9 Conscientious	
Raw Score	Percentile	Raw Score	Percentile	Raw Score	Percentile
0–5	0	0–5	0	0–8	0
6	4	6	3	9	1
7	9	7	5	10	2
8	18	8	9	11	4
9	31	9	13	12	5
10	42	10	22	13	7
11	53	11	31	14	10
12	61	12	41	15	16
13	66	13	46	16	23
14	73	14	53	17	30
15	80	15	60	18	38
16	83	16	67	19	46
17	87	17	71	20	56
18	92	18	77	21	70
19	95	19	82	22	79
20	97	20	86	23	88
21	98	21	88	24	92
22	99	22	91	25	100
23	100	23	92		
		24	94		
		25	98		
		26	99		
		27	100		

Scale 10 Achieving		Scale 11 Innovative	
Raw Score	Percentile	Raw Score	Percentile
0–15	0	0–13	0
16	1	14	1
17	2	16	2
18	3	17	4
19	4	18	6
20	5	19	12
21	8	20	16
22	13	21	25
23	19	22	35
24	26	23	47
25	38	24	56
26	52	25	65
27	63	26	75
28	76	27	82
29	88	28	91
30	100	29	96
		30	100

Example of Shaded ACT Profile

1. Helpfulness
2. Sociable
3. Need for Approval
4. Dependent
5. Tense
6. Rigid
7. Controlling
8. Competitive
9. Conscientious
10. Achieving
11. Innovative

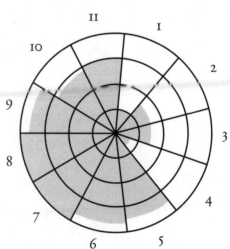

c . h . a . p . t . e . r   3

PROFILE LANDMARKS

Now that you have completed your assessment and reviewed your results, it's time to dig in and learn more about exactly what the ACT Profile measures. This will provide you with a better understanding of the ACT Profile in general and more important, offer you greater insight into the meaning of your specific assessment results.

The ACT Profile provides a snapshot of your personality. The assessment scales with the longest/largest shaded areas show which personality traits are most prominent and have the greatest impact on your behavior. The smaller shaded areas, that fall more to the center of the profile, represent personality traits that are less prominent in your overall personality makeup and have little influence on your behavior.

Scores for each of the personality traits are displayed in percentiles created from a database of scores from a cross section of professionals. The center point of the circle equals zero and the four concentric circles mark the twenty-fifth, fiftieth, seventy-fifth, and hundredth percentiles.

If you score 82 percent on Competitive, it means that 18 percent of people are more competitive than you are and 81 percent are less competitive. A score of 82 percent is a moderately high score compared to other people — higher than four out of five people. A score of 8 percent on Sociable indicates that 92 percent of people are more sociable than you are, and this is a relatively strong sign that you are not a people person.

How high or low your score is on a particular scale (e.g., 82 percent on Competitive, 8 percent on Sociable) is not good or bad, right or wrong; your percentage score on a particular scale simply reflects how much higher or lower your score is on that one scale compared to other people. Just as the psychology of personality is complex, so is the ACT Profile, and in part this complexity results from the fact that your personality traits interact with each other. Your score on an individual scale does not determine your effectiveness; what is important is the overall pattern in your profile and how this pattern matches the roles and responsibilities you have in your job and your aspirations.

So, if your score on Sociable is low, 8 percent, say, it is important to look also at your score on Helpfulness and to consider to what extent social skills are required in your job or for you to feel content and satisfied. For example, if you are in sales or customer service, a low score on Sociable accompanied by a low score on Helpfulness suggests a lack of the kinds of social skills needed for high performance in these jobs. If, on the other hand, you have a low score on Sociable but a high average score on Helpfulness (65 percent), it suggests that you are cooperative and have the collaborative attitude necessary to carry out the interpersonal aspects of your job. Low scores on both Sociable and Helpfulness may not matter as much for a software engineer who works very independently and is satisfied with limited social interactions. Every case is different.

That being said, research findings show that high scores on Conscientious, Achieving, Innovative, Helpfulness, and Sociable are generally associated with higher levels of performance, and high scores on Need for Approval, Dependent, Tense, Rigid, Controlling, and Competitive are generally associated with lower performance. The research that supports these findings will be explained in depth in the next chapter. The rest of this chapter will explain what each of the assessment scales measure, how each personality trait is important to performance on the job, and how the eleven assessment scales interact with one another and form groupings of scales that are commonly seen in people.

The ACT Scales

HELPFULNESS

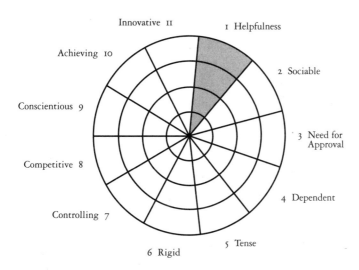

The Helpfulness scale is comprised of six assessment items: trusts others; patient; supportive and encouraging;

available to others; has concern for others; cooperative. Help-fulness measures interpersonal sensitivity, consensus build-ing, and an interest in working with and through others. The interpersonal skills assessed on the Helpfulness scale are key components of "emotional intelligence," which recent research has shown to be a strong predictor of effectiveness across many different kinds of professions.[1] Think about a person who has been encouraging and supportive to you, perhaps taken time to patiently teach you a new skill or helped you with a problem, and whose focus was on nurtur-ing your performance, not on their agenda. That is the type of person who scores high on the Helpfulness scale.

People who have high scores on Helpfulness are patient, good listeners, and use encouragement to motivate perfor-mance. High scores reflect a preference for teamwork, the presence of cooperation and collaboration skills, and a gen-erally optimistic view of others. In contrast, people with a low score on Helpfulness tend to be less interested in the welfare of others, are more self-absorbed and focused on their own needs, and tend to be less supportive, encouraging, and patient with others.

Studies show that the personality attributes measured on the Helpfulness scale are associated with high performance on the job.[2] Helpfulness is associated with excellence in *most* skill areas — from soft skills such as building relationships and listening to hard skills such as planning, quality im-provement, and problem solving. The reason that Helpful-ness is such a key asset is that people who are high in Helpfulness are open-minded, encourage open dialogue and the sharing of ideas, and have a positive outlook on things: key ingredients for teamwork, creativity, and high morale.

Can you have too much Helpfulness? In itself, Helpful-ness is an asset; and it is a great complement to results-oriented traits such as Controlling, Competitive, Conscientious, Achieving, and Innovative. Combined with a strong results orientation, Helpfulness brings warmth, a concern for others, and a supportive attitude that communicates to other people that they are important and valued. However, when combined with high scores on Need for Approval and Dependent, a high score on Helpfulness may indicate a person who is too nice and helpful to others, who sacrifices their own needs to serve others. They can have difficulties making decisions and getting results on their own due to their over-reliance on the participation of others.

SOCIABLE

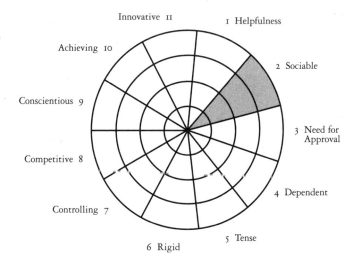

The Sociable scale includes six assessment items: likes meeting new people; develops positive relationships; gregarious and friendly; warmhearted; more open than reserved; loves to interact with others.

The Sociable scale measures your interest and ability in maintaining social relationships. Think of the person who seems to always wear a smile, says hello, and is friendly to everyone, and who obviously loves spending time with others, and you have described the person who will score high on the Sociable scale.

Sociable people like people, are friendly, warm, and interpersonally savvy. They tend to be energetic with others, enjoy group activities, and prefer a team environment to working on their own. Very sociable people derive great joy from socializing, actively seek out the company of others, and consider their relationships with friends and family a priority. Individuals who score low on the Sociable scale are much less motivated to develop or maintain relationships with other people and tend to be more private and reserved. People who score low on the Sociable scale are much more likely to be comfortable working independently than a highly sociable person who thrives on social contact and gets lonely when others are not around.

Sociability is associated with higher levels of effectiveness in the people-oriented professions, such as management, sales, and customer service.[3] Although sociability is not a consistently strong predictor of effectiveness in a person, a moderate degree of sociability is an asset when complemented by a drive for results. For example, a driven, results-oriented leader or manager with relationship skills builds trust and morale; the leader with an absence of these social skills may be perceived as self-absorbed and untrustworthy. Paying attention to the human side of the enterprise is essential for building motivation and trust.

Information-age workplaces demand teamwork skills and the ability to exchange ideas, so some social skills are needed. Perhaps even more important, sociable people report greater workplace satisfaction and more positive feelings about their employer and fellow employees than those who are short on sociability. The flip side is that sociability must be complemented by a strong results orientation for the work to get done. Sociability without discipline and a drive for results is a formula for a lack of productivity. Taking too much time for chitchat and not enough time to focus on work responsibilities and achieving goals won't get the job done.

NEED FOR APPROVAL

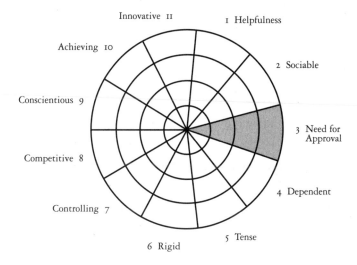

The Need for Approval scale is comprised of six assessment items: wants to please everyone; very concerned with what others think; works hard to be liked by others; needs to be liked by others; wants the approval of others; confrontational (confrontational is reverse scored, which means that people with a high need for approval are not confrontational).

This scale measures your interest in and drive to gain the favor and approval of others. People with a high need for approval place a priority on "getting along" and solicit assurance from others that things are "okay." Rebels do not score high on this scale.

Imagine a person who needs your constant assurances that you see them in a positive light. Perhaps they call your attention to the latest fashion piece they are wearing or tell you how they went out of their way to do a favor for someone, or remind you that they have some special talent. They tell you things that are intended to impress you, but you know they actually lack confidence and the reason that they tell you these things is to solicit your approval and reinforcement. They are needy. This may be an extreme example of how a person with a very high need for approval behaves, but there are many people in the world who not only seek out the approval of others but also seem to need it.

Now imagine a person in sales or a customer service position who appears to be genuinely focused on meeting your needs. They make strong efforts to gain your favor and are obviously concerned that you like them. They communicate that you are very important to them and that they are willing to do whatever it takes to satisfy your needs. This example sounds much more attractive, especially if you have experienced poor customer service where the service professional communicates that they do not value your regard and acceptance. This example illustrates why a moderate to high need for approval is an asset for a person in sales or customer service, especially when that person also has the focus and discipline required to get results.

People with a very high need for approval tend to be very generous, sometimes too generous. They will bend over backward to meet the needs of others, sometimes in spite of their own best interests and needs. People with a high need for approval compromise easily and are reluctant to take a firm stand, even when it would be appropriate. The person who is motivated by their need for approval will avoid disagreement and conflict — which can be an asset in sales or service positions but a liability in jobs where differences of opinion and disagreement are necessary and can lead to new, better outcomes

To operate effectively and to feel contented, the person with a strong need for approval must balance their need for pleasing and acquiescing to others with the resolve and discipline to get what they want and do what needs to be done.

DEPENDENT

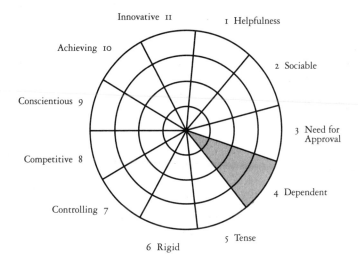

The Dependent scale includes the following six assessment items: not assertive; prefers to follow; defers to others; submissive; independent; has high standards (independent and has high standards are reverse scored; individuals who are very dependent typically would not say they are independent and tend to not set high standards).

The Dependent scale measures the need to look to others for direction and guidance. Hallmarks of this attribute are low assertiveness, appeasing others, and letting others make decisions. High scores on the Dependent scale reflect a preference to be compliant, to maintain the status quo, and to play it safe. These preferences conflict with the high premium of many professional positions in today's global marketplace on the ability to foster and deal with change. On the other hand, for positions that require close adherence to already established guidelines and procedures, and where following precedent is key, a person who is dependent will feel comfortable where more independent thinking people will not.

Dependent people tend to have low initiative, are self-doubting, and do not like to be placed in a position of leadership. They would rather follow the lead of others. For these reasons, high scores on the Dependent scale are associated with a lower level of performance on the job.[4] Highly dependent people feel at the mercy of events: events happen to them. They have an external locus of control. They react to events rather than make things happen. In contrast, people with a low score on Dependent are more likely to have an internal locus of control: they apply personal intention and effort to make events happen. A low score on Dependent reflects the presence of initiative, a higher level of self-confidence, and a preference to assume responsibilities rather than follow the lead of others.

While the highly dependent person is neither assertive nor proactive, their mild manner and willingness to work hard and follow the direction of a leader make them important members of a team. Highly dependent people are often happy to just fit in, to quietly go about their work, and they seldom create conflicts or controversy. They are tactful, modest, and have respect for rules and regulations. They are loyal to individuals and to organizations that have supported and encouraged their efforts. I've worked with very capable, highly dependent managers at top levels of Fortune 500 companies who provide exactly what is needed on an executive team where the other, more charismatic team members create conflicts and ill will as they battle for power and control.

TENSE

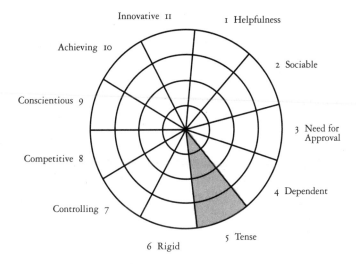

The Tense scale is comprised of four assessment items: tense and uneasy; apprehensive and unsure; insecure, lacks self-confidence; calm and collected (calm and collected is reverse scored, which means that people who are tense are not calm and collected)

The Tense scale measures the tendency to worry and feel anxious. Some anxiety and apprehension are part of the human condition and function to keep us alert, but very tense people are often unhappy. They are pessimistic and see problems rather than opportunities. Some of these problems may be quite real and appropriately demand time and attention to solve, but highly tense people also worry about many problems and negative outcomes that never actually develop. As a result, tension ruins many a good day for those who worry about worst-case scenarios that never occur. The character that Woody Allen plays in his movies is a good example of a very tense person.

People who score high on the Tense scale tend to experience periods of self-doubt and apprehension. While most people have experienced butterflies before an important event like a speech or major sales presentation, those who score high on the Tense scale may suffer prolonged periods of nervousness and anxiety. In addition, tension interacts with other attitudes and behaviors, so the specific way that it gets expressed is strongly influenced by the other ACT scales that are prominent in a profile. For example, being tense can further inhibit the shy person or push an aggressive, results-oriented person into being bossy and overaggressive. Regardless of the other personality traits in a profile, research studies indicate that high scores on the Tense scale are associated with decreased performance on the job.[5] In 1999, productivity losses from anxiety in the workplace totaled more than $37 billion.[6]

Current research suggests that in some people there is a biological basis for high levels of tension and apprehension, and new medications are being used to help people who experience long-term, unremitting anxiety. Exercise, meditation, relaxation techniques, biofeedback, and psychotherapy are also effective approaches to reduce levels of tension.

RIGID

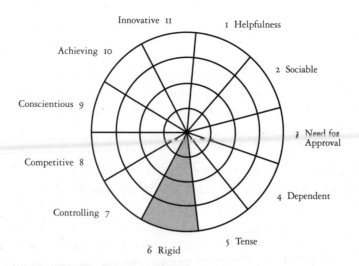

The Rigid scale has six assessment items: narrow-minded; does not listen; inflexible; stubborn; mistrustful; open-minded (open-minded is reverse scored because people who are rigid tend to have a low score on this assessment item).

This scale measures the tendency to be inflexible, stubborn, and resistant to new ideas. A very rigid person has strong opinions and is not willing to entertain alternative points of view. Rigid thinkers enjoy arguments and debates and ask lots of questions. They like playing the devil's advocate and tend to focus on finding problems rather than solutions.

Some of the characteristics measured on the Rigid scale are helpful in moderation, because people who have an average level of rigid thinking are discriminating, do not take things at face value, and are not easily fooled. On the other hand, the total absence of the characteristics measured on the Rigid scale can be problematic. A person with a very low score on the Rigid scale may have no strong opinions and lack a level of skepticism that could help uncover the truth about a situation.

> *Nothing will ever be attempted if all possible objections must first be overcome.*
> — Samuel Johnson

But high scores on the Rigid scale are associated with decreased performance on the job.[7] People who are very rigid are difficult to have as a teammate. Have you ever spent time with a person who responds to each and every suggestion you make by finding fault with your ideas because they do not fit their more narrowly defined view of the world? Whether it is a new way to present an old product, a suggestion on what restaurant to go to, brainstorming new ideas to streamline your business processes, why you like Hawaii as a vacation destination — the topic seems not to matter. People who score high on the Rigid scale tend to oppose and find something wrong with almost anything you suggest.

It is no surprise that a professional whose profile reflects a strong rigidity component is likely to experience difficulties in social and work situations. Such a person is perceived as contrary, stubborn, argumentative, and a poor listener. In a work setting, rigidity impedes creativity and stifles open communication by focusing on what is wrong with new ideas rather than building on what is right.

CONTROLLING

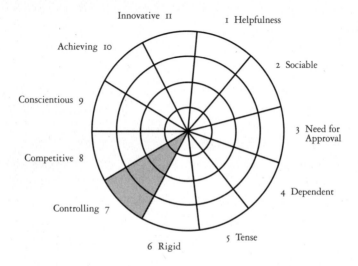

The Controlling scale is composed of six assessment items: self-centered, egotistical; bossy, dictatorial; forceful, pushy; criticizes others; controlling, dominating; expresses confidence in others (this last item is reverse scored because controlling people rarely express confidence in others and tend rather to be critical of others).

The Controlling scale measures the tendency to be authoritarian, adversarial, and aggressive. In moderation, the characteristics measured by the Controlling scale are expressed in positive behaviors such as assertiveness, a willingness to form opinions and take a stand, and decisiveness. People with moderate controlling tendencies like to have responsibilities and influence and to make an impact. They get involved in their work, are passionate about their values and beliefs, and are willing to work very hard in pursuit of their goals.

People who score high on the Controlling scale feel a need to dominate situations and exercise their power and influence, using a forceful, bossy approach. They are very opinionated and tend to take a narrow view of things, often also scoring high on the Rigid scale. People with a high score on the Controlling scale are very direct in stating their opinions, thus lacking in tact and diplomacy, which are important for maintaining good interpersonal relationships. They tend to be insensitive about others' feelings and may say or do things that are hurtful. Although controlling people tend to go on the offensive, they also are quite defensive and easily offended when they do not think others are according them appropriate status and respect. They take things personally and make things personal — a counterproductive style for teamwork. Controlling people have difficulty cooperating. It is not surprising that there is a large body of research that shows that people who score high on the Controlling scale are less effective on the job.[8]

Controlling people generally are impatient and feel a sense of urgency to do it now. They do not like extensive planning, and those with very high scores have a tendency to be impulsive. They prefer a "ready-shoot-aim" approach. They also have a quick temper and get very bothered when things do not go the way they want. Very controlling people have a high level of hostility, which the latest research identifies as *the* mortality component in type A behavior. An aggressive, controlling style is not only hard on other people but also stressful on oneself.

> *Anyone can become angry — that is easy. But to be angry with the right person, to the right degree, at the right time, for the right purpose, and in the right way — this is not easy.*
> — Aristotle

COMPETITIVE

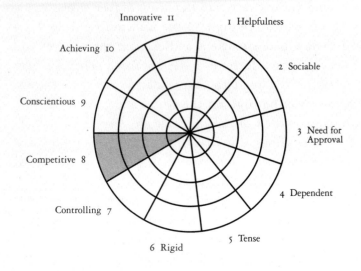

Innovative 11

1 Helpfulness

Achieving 10

2 Sociable

Conscientious 9

3 Need for Approval

Competitive 8

4 Dependent

Controlling 7

5 Tense

6 Rigid

The Competitive scale includes six assessment items: works to outdo others; makes everything a competition; measures success by wins; brags about winning; lets everyone know who won and who lost; needs to bury the competition.

This scale measures the need to compete with and outdo other people. While many forms of competition are totally appropriate and healthy, this scale measures the tendency to compete to an extreme and to set up win-lose situations rather than create win-win scenarios. The ability to create win-win scenarios is essential for collaboration and cooperation.

Very competitive people tend to also have high scores on the Need for Approval scale. Many people compete incessantly because they feel a strong need to gain the approval and regard of others, often to compensate for feelings of insecurity. Consider a person who seems compelled to continually tell you of their successes and wins, of how great they are. They crave attention and are self-centered, seeming to be able to focus only on their own performance rather than considering and valuing the contributions of others. The impression they create is often of neediness — needing you to tell them that they are important and deserve your high regard. It sounds like "me, me, me" and is off-putting, because other people appreciate humility and teamwork and tire of an individual who must constantly vie to be the center of attention.

Even professional athletes need to understand that being competitive is only productive to a point. Gary Payton, the all-star guard on the Seattle Supersonics, has always been well respected for his basketball skills. But, until Payton was able to temper his competitiveness and be more of a team player, his leadership ability was compromised and his relationship with his teammates was rocky. As his teammate Vin Baker said, "In the past Gary would let his competitiveness override his intelligence. . . . He was always the best point guard physically; now he's become the best point guard mentally."[9] Payton's willingness to control his competitiveness and consciously focus on behaving as a better teammate is an example that some businesspeople need to follow. Most businesses operate as teams, and team members must count on others to focus on team wins — not individual victories. Focusing on outdoing others and being the winner means that some others must be losers. This is not a good strategy for either cooperatively working with or motivating others toward collaboration and high performance.

Not surprisingly, some competitiveness, especially when accompanied by social skills, is an asset in sales. Salespeople are constantly competing against other products and salespeople to win the sale. And their compensation often is directly tied to wins and losses. But the most effective salespeople complement a competitive style with a focus on high achievement, and show empathy and a strong service orientation that keep their focus on satisfying customer needs.[10]

CONSCIENTIOUS

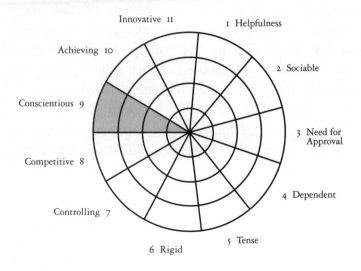

The Conscientious scale is comprised of six assessment items: disciplined; detail oriented; careful, precise; does things right; does not plan ahead; disorganized (these latter two items are reverse scored; people who are conscientious are organized and plan ahead).

This scale measures the need to produce high-quality results, to attend to details, and to want to do things the right way the first time. Conscientious people focus on their job and work very hard to achieve quality results, and, as expected, professionals who are conscientious tend to be more effective on the job.[11] High scores on the Conscientious scale are associated with attributes including perseverance, being organized, and wanting responsibility. People who score high are dedicated to doing whatever it takes to get the job done. At the extremes, however, conscientiousness can be problematic. Too much conscientiousness can lead to perfectionism and a sense that "good enough never is." This can create stress and discontentment. Too little conscientiousness, on the other hand, points to an absence of attention to details and a lack of discipline. Very low scores on the Conscientious scale are associated with not setting high standards, taking a casual approach to work, and sloppiness. High scores on the Achieving scale, which measures ambition and the enjoyment of challenges, can often make up for some of the shortcomings associated with a low level of conscientiousness. A low score on the Conscientious scale and a high score on the Achieving scale usually indicate a person who is willing to work hard, enjoys work, but is not particularly well organized or detail oriented.

The Conscientious scale is a chameleon scale, being strongly colored by what other ACT scales are prominent in the profile (You will see this again in the Domineering and Effectiveness Sectors on pages 52 and 53). A high score on Conscientious accompanied by high scores on Rigid, Controlling, and Competitive is a formula for a discontented, aggressive micromanager. In contrast, a high score on Conscientious in concert with high scores on Achieving, Innovation, and Helpfulness form the basis of a highly effective profile.

ACHIEVING

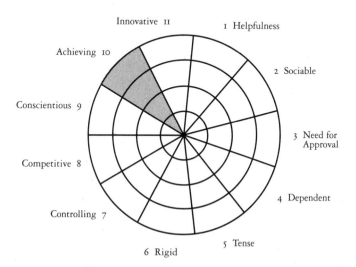

The Achieving scale contains six assessment items: ambitious; likes challenges; enjoys work; aspires to excel; likes to learn; content with the status quo (content with the status quo is reverse scored: high achievers are not content with the status quo).

This scale measures interest in working on and enjoying challenging tasks. High achievers are ambitious, self-directed, and enjoy intellectually challenging projects. They are passionate about their ideas and their work. High achievers actively seek out opportunities to exercise their judgment, skills, and abilities. They are pragmatic and realistic, optimistic about things, set "stretch" goals, and have clear ideas about their standards of excellence.

People who score high on the Achieving scale have an internal locus of control, believing that their personal efforts have an impact on the outcome of events. They tend to be goal oriented and like to be active. Redundant activities or repetitive work that allows them little opportunity to use their thinking skills bores them. They like to be in a position of leadership, and high scores on the Achieving scale are closely associated with leadership and professional effectiveness. Individuals with high scores on Achieving are rated as the most productive and effective workers — across industries and professions. Research studies consistently show that a high need for achievement is strongly related to success and satisfaction at work.[12]

Individuals with strong achievement orientations but without complementary social skills may strike others as too focused on their work and their own ideas. A high need for achievement is generally directed into projects and tasks, not focused on people. An individual who has high scores on the Achieving, Rigid, Controlling, and Competitive scales may be a relentless worker, driven to succeed, and may in fact be very accomplished in their work, but they also may be self-absorbed, abrupt, and behave insensitively toward others. This type of person may be successful in getting results but feel dissatisfied because of a lack of good personal relationships. Like all the traits measured by the ACT Profile, the way that a person's achievement orientations is expressed is colored by the other traits that are prominent in their profile.

INNOVATIVE

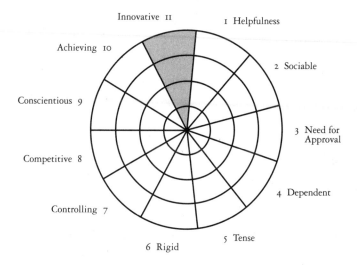

The six assessment items that make up the Innovative scale are: clever; confident; generates new ideas; imaginative, creative; inquisitive, curious about things; prefers a low-risk approach (prefers a low-risk approach is reverse scored, as innovative people are willing to take risks).

This scale measures an individual's inventiveness, inquisitiveness, curiosity, and confidence in trying new things. Innovative people are independent minded and have a strong sense of commitment and satisfaction. They are interested in learning and seek out situations to develop their interests and knowledge. They are enthusiastic and highly motivated to turn possibilities into realities. As a result, the characteristics measured on the Innovative scale are associated with higher performance and satisfaction on the job.[13]

High scores on the Innovative scale indicate creativity and confidence and usually nonconformity. People who score high on this scale deal well with change, are flexible, secure, and are upbeat. They often have a wide range of interests and are bored by routine tasks. Individuals who score low on the Innovative scale generally prefer a low-risk approach to things, are not particularly comfortable with change, and like things to be consistent and predictable.

You can compare your scores on the Innovative scale with your scores on the Tense scale for a measure of your overall sense of security, optimism, and satisfaction.

360-Degree Assessments

The 360-degree assessments, also known as multi-rater assessments, are commonly used in corporations in management and leadership development programs. In a 360-degree assessment, the participant completes a self-assessment and also collects feedback from coworkers — subordinates, peers, managers, and sometimes customers or vendors. The advantage of 360-degree assessments is that participants are able to compare their self-perceptions with feedback that shows how others perceive them. Some people have great insight into how others perceive them and some people have no idea. As workshop leaders say, "You may think you are walking on water and find that others think you're passing it."

There are two kinds of 360-degree assessments: those that measure personality traits like those measured on the ACT Profile (the 360-degree version of the ACT Profile is called MAP*11*) and those that measure discrete, work-related skills such as planning, organizing, performance feedback, staff development, or teamwork. This latter type of 360-degree assessment is called a competency assessment and is used in a vast majority of Fortune 1000 corporations.

Competencies equate to what people do and personality equates to how they do it. Personality and competencies are related. For instance, Evelyn has training and skills in quality improvement and is perceptive and articulate around quality methods. However, her personality style causes her to aggressively criticize current methods and to appear uninterested in helping others discover new ways to raise quality, so her competencies in quality improvement are compromised by aspects of her personality. Thus, it is not just what you know and what you can do but also how you do it.

Women managers score higher than their male counterparts on

(continued)

360-Degree Assessments (*continued*)

360-degree competency assessments of management and leadership skills (despite the fact that men provide the bulk of the feedback ratings). Women score higher on soft skills such as relationship skills and staff development, and on hard skills such as planning and problem solving.

These findings may suggest that women are more skilled than men on these job competencies or, more likely, may reflect the invisible "glass ceiling" that requires that women perform at a higher skill level than men in order to be promoted to management and leadership positions.

Studies show that work performance improves when people receive 360-degree assessment feedback, and individuals who have the greatest skill deficits benefit the most.[14]

The Arrangement of the Personality Traits on the ACT Profile

The eleven ACT scales are positioned within the profile to reflect the interrelationships between the scales. Scales that are adjacent to one another are most related to each other. For example, Helpfulness and Sociable are next to each other and these two traits measure positive aspects of interpersonal skills. Generally, people who score high on Helpfulness tend to also score high on Sociable. Likewise, Controlling and Rigid are next to each other and these two scales thus measure attributes that are closely related. In general, people who are controlling also tend to be rigid.

Personality traits on opposite sides of the ACT Profile (in general) measure personality attributes that are opposites. For instance, Helpfulness and Controlling are opposites on the profile and they are opposites behaviorally as well. Someone who is helpful is generally open-minded, patient, and encouraging of others. Someone who is controlling tends to be inflexible, impatient, and critical of others. These are opposite sets of behaviors and are so depicted in the layout of the profile.

Sectors of the ACT Profile

Since adjacent scales are more related to one another than scales in other parts of the profile, there are distinct areas or sectors within the profile that measure related dimensions of behavior. For instance, you may have noticed that Helpfulness, Sociable, Need for Approval, and Dependent all measure attitudes and behaviors associated with interpersonal relationships. Or that the Rigid, Controlling, and Competitive scales are associated with behaviors that can be described as egocentric or self-absorbed. You may have also noticed that all the ACT Profile scales toward the top of the profile, the Achieving, Innovative, Helpfulness, and Sociable scales, are associated with high performance.

Thus, the areas on the right, left, top, and bottom of the profile are all distinctive. The scales on the right side of the ACT Profile measure traits associated with social orientations (Helpfulness, Sociable, Need for Approval, Dependent). The scales on the left side of the profile measure traits associated with task orientations (Controlling, Competitive, Conscientious, Achieving, Innovative). The scales at the top of the profile measure traits associated with high performance at work (Conscientious, Achieving, Innovative, Helpfulness, Sociable). The scales at the bottom of the profile measure traits associated with decreased effectiveness at work (Need for Approval, Dependent, Tense, Rigid, Controlling, Competitive).

Additionally, there are three main sectors in the ACT Profile: Deferential, Domineering, and Effectiveness.

THE DEFERENTIAL SECTOR

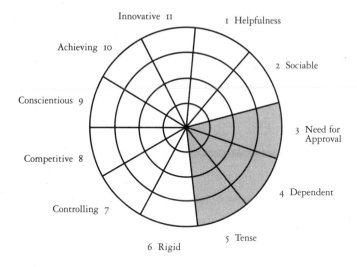

The Need for Approval, Dependent, and Tense scales, as a group, form the Deferential sector. This sector is associated with unassertive, deferential, passive behavior. High scores in this sector reflect a preference for letting others take the lead, being agreeable, and avoiding confrontation. Depending on what other traits are prominent in a profile and the job roles and responsibilities, this complex of traits can be an asset or a liability. For example, if you are a customer service representative who must establish a supportive and patient rapport with customers and closely follow procedures for solving problems, high scores in the Deferential sector accompanied by high scores on the Helpfulness and Sociable scales can be an effective profile. On the other hand, if you are a manager that must develop new ways to solve problems in an environment with few procedures, the attitudes and behaviors associated with the Deferential sector will be a liability (even if complemented by high scores on Helpfulness and Sociable).

THE DOMINEERING SECTOR

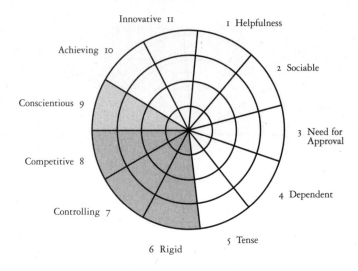

The Rigid, Controlling, Competitive, and Conscientious scales — as a grouping — create the Domineering sector. This sector reflects a very independent, dominating, and inflexible style. One of the most frequent profiles seen in the general population — if not one of the most popular types — is an ACT Profile with high scores in the Domineering sector. An individual with very high scores in the Domineering sector often feels a need to prove him- or herself by controlling events, seeking results independently, and feeling important through mastery of projects and tasks. Individuals with their highest scores in this sector feel a need to be right and to turn things into competitions, complete with winners and losers. These individuals are very assertive and have strong needs to be viewed by others as competent, admitting to no doubts, weaknesses, or vulnerabilities. People with their highest scores in the Domineering sector tend to see things as either black or white, with no gray or middle area. They have very strong beliefs about things and tend to not be open to other views and interpretations.

THE EFFECTIVENESS SECTOR

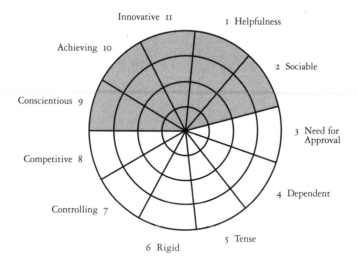

Many studies cited in this chapter have shown that the traits and behaviors measured by the Conscientious, Achieving, Innovative, Helpfulness, and Sociable scales are associated with effectiveness on the job.

The Effectiveness sector contains the traits associated with a well-balanced person who has initiative, intellectual and emotional flexibility, patience, and social skills. Individuals with very high scores in the Effectiveness sector are confident but not cocky, assertive but not overaggressive, open-minded, and willing to listen. The traits in the Effectiveness sector are associated with high performance — regardless of the profession. That is why these traits are considered desirable on employee selection tests, training and development assessments, and sometimes even on performance appraisals. As reported in chapter 4, studies of commercial airline pilots by the National Aeronautics and Space Administration (NASA), the Federal Aviation Administration (FAA), and the National Transportation Safety Board (NTSB) indicate that cockpit crews led by captains with a high need for achievement and strong social skills make the fewest errors.

A study reported in the *Harvard Business Review* found that 90 percent of managers waste time due to inefficiencies that are created by their personal work styles. In the study, conducted by Heike Bruch, a professor of leadership at the University of St. Gallen in Switzerland, and Sumantra Ghoshal, a professor of strategy and international management at the London Business School, it was revealed that 40 percent of managers are "distracted," 30 percent are "procrastinators," and 20 percent are "disengaged," leaving only 10 percent who do not waste time and are "purposeful."[15] These distinct types of inefficiency bear some similarities to particular sectors in the ACT Profile.

Distracted managers have a high level of energy and little focus. They are impulsive, and even when the best strategy is to wait and carefully analyze a situation, they tend to act or react immediately. Distracted managers show a similar behavior style to that characteristic of the Domineering sector.

Procrastinators have neither the focus nor the energy for high performance. They prefer routine tasks such as attending meetings and writing memos, but lack the initiative and drive required for high performance. Procrastinators show some of the same behavior styles that are characteristic of the Deferential sector.

Disengaged managers are very focused but lack the energy to get the job done. They do not see a purpose in their work and will use psychological defenses like denial to simply ignore the work that needs to get done. These managers share some of the behavioral characteristics seen in a combination of the Domineering and Deferential sectors.

Finally, Bruch and Ghoshal identified purposeful managers who have the focus, energy, and initiative to take on and accomplish important tasks. These managers show some of the key characteristics of the Conscientious, Achieving, and Innovative scales that make up the results-oriented components of the Effectiveness sector.

Profile Characteristics in the General Population

Most people have high scores in one or two profile sectors. This is consistent with the fact that most people have some traits that contribute to their effectiveness and some traits that get in the way. About one out of four professionals has a self-profile with an overwhelming predominance of traits in the Effectiveness sector and very low scores on the other ACT traits. For most people, the key to their self-development is to learn to fully utilize the personality styles that are natural strengths and to learn to manage personality shortcomings and weaknesses that get in the way of high performance.

To understand how central a role personality has at work, the following chapter introduces you to some of the latest thinking about how and why personality can be an asset or a liability in the workplace. It discusses which specific personality traits can augment or compromise your other talents, and what traits are important for what types of jobs. Examples are provided that range from the more routine (managers, line professionals, salespeople) to the unusual (commercial airline pilots), all of which illustrate that there are more common denominators in the set of personality traits associated with high performance across professions than there are major differences.

Notes

1. Daniel Goleman, *Emotional Intelligence* (New York: Bantam Books, 1995).

2. Fred Hertzberg, *The Motivation to Work* (New York: John Wiley & Sons, 1959); Douglas McGregor, *The Human Side of Enterprise* (New York: McGraw-Hill, 1960); Rensis Likert, *The Human Organization* (New York: McGraw-Hill, 1967); Peter Gratzinger, Ronald Warren, and Robert Cooke, "Psychological Orientation and Leadership: Thinking Styles That Differentiate between Effective and Ineffective Managers." in *Measures of Leadership,* ed. Kenneth Clark and Miriam Clark (Greensboro, N.C.: Center for Creative Leadership, 1990); Herb Greenberg, Harold Weinstein, and Patrick Sweeney, *How to Hire and Develop Your Next Top Performer* (New York: McGraw-Hill, 2001).

3. David McClelland, *The Achieving Society* (New York: The Free Press, 1976); John Kotter, *The Leadership Factor* (New York: The Free Press, 1988); Edward Hoffman, *Psychological Testing at Work* (New York: McGraw-Hill, 2002); Greenberg, Weinstein, and Sweeney, *How to Hire and Develop Your Next Top Performer.*

4. Gratzinger, Warren, and Cooke, "Psychological Orientations and Leadership: Thinking Styles That Differentiate between Effective and Ineffective Managers," (1990).

5. Ibid.

6. *The Journal of Clinical Psychiatry,* 1999.

7. Gratzinger, Warren, and Cooke, "Psychological Orientation and Leadership: Thinking Styles That Differentiate between Effective and Ineffective Managers."; Goleman, *Emotional Intelligence.*

8. Gratzinger, Warren, and Cooke, "Psychological Orientation and Leadership: Thinking Styles That Differentiate between Effective and Ineffective Managers."; Goleman, *Emotional Intelligence;* Hertzberg, *The Motivation to Work.*

9. *Sports Illustrated,* 7 January 2002.

10. Greenberg, Weinstein, and Sweeney, *How to Hire and Develop Your Next Top Performer.*

11. Robert Hogan and Joyce Hogan, *Hogan Personality Inventory Manual,* 2d ed. (Tulsa, Okla.: Hogan Assessment Systems, 1995); Paul Costa and Robert McCrae, *Bibliography for the Revised NEO Personality Inventory and NEO Five Factor Inventory* (Odessa, Fla.: Psychological Assessment Resources, 1994); Jean Brittain Leslie and John Fleenor, *Feedback to Managers* (Greensboro, N.C.: Center for Creative Leadership, 1998); Paul Costa and Robert McCrae, *Manual Supplement for the NEO 4* (Odessa, Fla.: Psychological Assessment Resources, 1994); Greenberg, Weinstein, and Sweeney, *How to Hire and Develop Your Next Top Performer;* McClelland, *The Achieving Society;* Kotter, *The Leadership Factor.*

12. McClelland, *The Achieving Society;* Leslie and Fleenor, *Feedback to Managers;* Gratzinger, Warren, and Cooke, "Psychological Orientation and Leadership: Thinking Styles That Differentiate between Effective and Ineffective Managers."; Hogan and Hogan, *Hogan Personality Inventory Manual;* Costa and McCrae, *Bibliography for the Revised NEO Personality Inventory and NEO Five Factor Inventory;* Costa and McCrae, *Manual Supplement for the NEO 4;* Greenberg, Weinstein, and Sweeney, *How to Hire and Develop Your Next Top Performer.*

13. Noel Tichy and Mary Ann Devanna, *The Transformational Leader* (New York: John Wiley & Sons, 1986); Gratzinger, Warren, and Cooke, "Psychological Orientation and Leadership: Thinking Styles That Differentiate between Effective and Ineffective Managers."; Costa and McCrae, *Bibliography for the Revised NEO Personality Inventory and NEO Five Factor Inventory;* Costa and McCrae, *Manual Supplement for the NEO 4;* Leslie and Fleenor, *Feedback to Managers.*

14. J. F. Hazucha, J. A. Gentile, and J. A. Schneider, "The Impact of 360-Degree Feedback on Management Skills Development," *Human Resource Management* 32 (1993): 325–352.

15. Heike Bruch and Sumantra Ghoshal, "Beware the Busy Manager," *Harvard Business Review* (February 2002).

c . h . a . p . t . e . r   4

PERSONALITY AT WORK

You have now completed your ACT Self-Profile, studied your assessment results, and, in the previous chapter, read about the ACT Profile and what it measures. In this chapter you will learn about personality traits that are associated with high performance and those that are counterproductive and impede effectiveness and satisfaction at work. I also introduce research on the relationship of personality to performance across a wide range of professions, and, toward the chapter's end, I focus on commercial aviation in particular, where, as you will see, the relationship between personality and performance on the job sometimes plays out dramatically.

The high premium that corporations place on leadership, management, and teamwork skills can represent a personal asset or liability for you. Whether you are looking for a job or are currently employed, if you are committed to skillfully managing your career, you must also be dedicated to managing your personality. You have already taken the first steps toward managing your personality by completing your assessment and studying the results. The next step is to understand which traits are associated with high performance and which are counterproductive.

The Success Traits and Counterproductive Traits

High performers share a set of characteristics that set them apart: they are optimistic, hardworking, ambitious, open-minded, patient, and encouraging. They work well both independently and on teams. On the ACT Profile, they score high on five traits: Conscientious, Achieving, Innovative, Helpfulness, and Sociable.

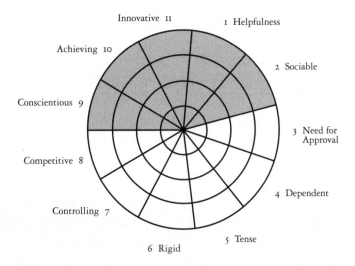

A large body of research supports the assertion that these five traits are associated with high performance across a spectrum of different jobs, industries, and demographics (gender, race, age).[1] Although the traits might be labeled differently — Sociable is sometimes called "affiliation" or "gregariousness" or "relationship skills" — the attitudes and behaviors embodied by these terms have a huge impact on job success and satisfaction. I will refer to these five traits in the ACT Profile as the success traits.

Very few individuals — only about 15 percent — have all the success traits unaccompanied by any prominent counterproductive traits, but for those who do, it is this rare combination of all the success traits that leads to the highest levels of effectiveness, success, and satisfaction. Most people have at least one or several of the success traits, usually in combination with counterproductive personality attributes that interfere with performance and satisfaction.

Research studies also support the idea that five counterproductive traits measured in the ACT Profile — Need for Approval, Dependent, Tense, Rigid, and Controlling — are present in most of us and have a major role in undermining effectiveness and satisfaction in the workplace (see discussion on Competitiveness that follows on page 61). Robert Hogan, a professor of psychology at the University of Oklahoma, says that shyness, indecisiveness, apprehension, over-aggressiveness, arrogance, and self-absorption are so common and undermine performance so much that they are the leading cause of managerial incompetence.

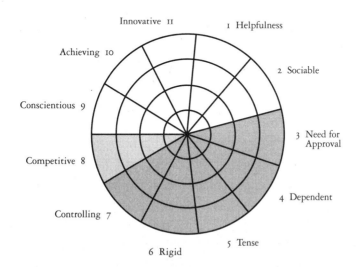

In a 1997 study of 511 company leaders, Richard Hagberg found that 70 percent were "loners," dangerously insulated from other team members. These leaders were intellectually and technically skilled, but also self-absorbed, impatient, impulsive, manipulative, dominating, and critical of others. They lacked insight into their strengths and weaknesses and were abusive to others in the workplace. Hagberg recounts the story of a CEO impatiently waiting in line with his wife to renew his driver's license. He becomes infuriated at how long it is taking to get served and says to his wife, "I have a lot to do. Don't they know who I am?" She replies, "Yeah, you're a plumber's son who got lucky." His wife's comment gave him an abrupt insight into his outsized sense of self-importance — a self-importance and sense of entitlement that caused him, and others, difficulties in and out of work.

On the ACT Profile, the traits that Hogan describes are represented as follows: shyness by very low scores on the Sociable and Helpfulness scales; indecisiveness by high scores on the Dependent scale; apprehension by a high mark on the Tense scale; and overaggressiveness by high scores on the Controlling scale.

It is important to remember three things about counterproductive traits:

1. In moderation, none of these traits interferes with success or satisfaction.

2. Traits do not operate in a vacuum; they interact with and are influenced by the presence of the other prominent characteristics. The impact of a counterproductive (or success) trait is heightened or diminished by the presence of other prominent traits in your profile. For example, consider Dale and Chris, who both have a high score on the Rigid scale. Dale also has high scores on the Tense, Controlling, and Competitive scales. Chris, by contrast, has high scores on the Achieving, Innovative, and Helpfulness scales. Dale has strong opinions, behaves in a stubborn, self-centered manner,

and is not interested in others' views and perspectives. Chris has strong opinions, but is intellectually flexible, is willing to change his mind for a good reason, and will actively seek input from others.

3. Competitiveness is counterproductive for some jobs and associated with high performance in other jobs. For example, very competitive managers diminish their effectiveness because a manager's job is to make those they manage successful by providing recognition and rewards and focusing on team performance. Very competitive managers tend to come across as self-absorbed and competitiveness interferes with essential team-leader skills. In contrast, salespeople who have a competitive nature accompanied by the success traits tend to be higher performers than those who are not competitive. At the same time, salespeople who are competitive but lack the success traits tend not to be high performers.

Signal versus Noise

Personality modulates the other forms of human capital that people bring to the workplace. The success traits do not independently make people successful; they help people use their intelligence, education, experience, and technical skills more effectively. I like to use the signal-to-noise model borrowed from electronics to help illustrate this modulation concept. Think of your role in your job as that of transmitting a signal (using your knowledge) for your employer. Your goal, and your employer's goal, is to have you transmit the purest signal, and to generate the least noise. The success traits facilitate your transmission of that signal and make it easier for you to utilize your other talents and abilities. Counterproductive personality attributes not only interfere with the signal but also generate noise — static — further eroding the potential for a good transmission and reception of the signal.

Take Ed as an example of a typical individual with some success

(continued)

Signal versus Noise (continued)

traits — signal — and some counterproductive tendencies — noise. Ed is very bright and has several advanced degrees. He is hardworking, motivated, ambitious, has an eye for detail, likes people, and is willing to go out of his way to help others. On the ACT Profile, Ed has high scores on the Conscientious, Achieving, Helpfulness, and Sociable scales. Sounds great: the presence of several success traits suggests that Ed would be a fabulous person to have on your team. Except that Ed also has very high scores on the Need for Approval, Controlling, and Competitive scales. As a result, Ed is constantly competing with others, trying to outdo them, but because of his sociability and high need for approval, he tries to do this in a friendly and sometimes covert manner. For example, it is not uncommon for Ed to give out a compliment like, "Jill is one of the strongest people on the finance team," but then add, "You know, I have an MBA and spent twelve years in a financial institution; it's one of my areas of talent, too. I try to help Jill out all that I can, but she's pretty capable." Ed compliments others so that he then can describe how he is even more talented than the person he complimented. This would be more tolerable if Ed also did not seem compelled to tell you how talented he is in everything ("I'm a very serious jogger. If you need some tips, I'd be happy to help." "I've been helping out in HR because I think some of our folks are raising issues that may be a bit too sophisticated for Jack. I mean, Jack is great, but some of these delicate issues are beyond him. He's young. . . . It's not what I really like doing, but I guess I'm just good at it. People are comfortable talking to me about their conflicts. You know, I studied psychology in college." "I'd love to help you out on the Acme project. I know that you are our expert in that type of analysis, but I'm interested in that type of work too and am good at it. Did I ever tell you about my work in that area?" "What kind of music do you like? You know, I play guitar and consider myself something of a musician."). So Ed is a classic example of someone with success traits and counterproductive tendencies. Ed does not need to develop more ambition or to become more patient, but he does need to manage his need for approval and his competitiveness for others to feel good about working with him. His need to always be one step ahead of the rest gets old and is draining for those around him. Ed has told me so many times about his MBA that I've come to think it stands for "most bragged about."

Research on Personality and Job Effectiveness

During the past twenty years, I have conducted many studies on personality and job performance. In one of the first studies, managers who ranked in the top 10 percent of effectiveness had self-profiles dominated by success traits, with high scores on traits measuring Achieving, Innovative, Helpfulness, and

Most-Effective Managers 1996 Study

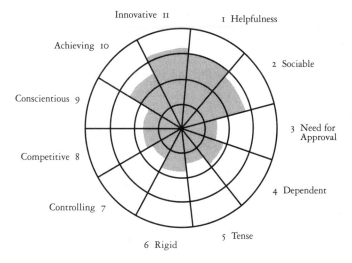

Least-Effective Managers 1996 Study

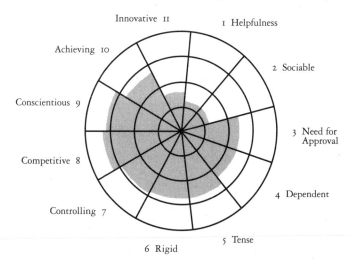

Sociable and low scores on the counterproductive traits. Managers who ranked in the lowest 10 percent of effectiveness had self-profiles dominated by counterproductive traits and very low scores on the success traits. These profile

Most-Effective Managers 2000 Study

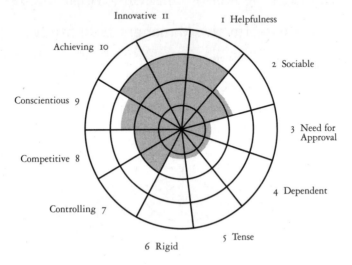

Least-Effective Managers 2000 Study

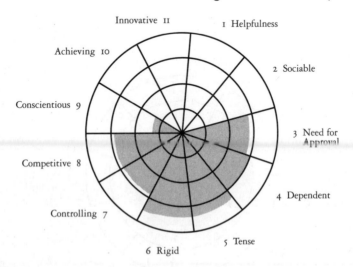

differences were even more dramatic in the 360-degree results (see chapter 3 for a discussion of 360-degree assessments), as seen in the profiles on page 63.[2]

Similar patterns of results have been found in other studies, including some that link personality traits to team performance in business simulations, promotions, pay, and stress
tolerance.[3] In a 1996 study, several thousand professionals
completed a self-profile and were rated by over ten thousand
coworkers on their personality traits and job performance.
Professionals who ranked in the top 10 percent scored high on
the success traits and had low scores on the counterproductive
traits in both their self-profiles and 360-degree behavior ratings.[4] This same pattern of results was seen in a 2001 study
using a 360-degree version of the ACT Profile — MAP*11* —
as shown in the profiles on pages 64–66.[5]

Most-Effective Professionals 2000 Study

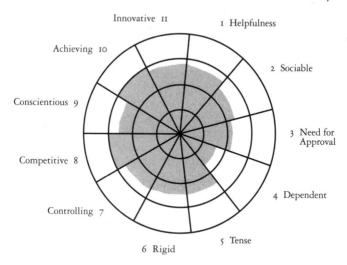

Least-Effective Professionals 2000 Study

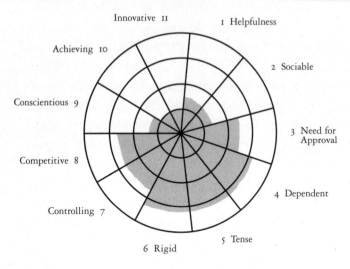

Innovative 11   1 Helpfulness
Achieving 10
Conscientious 9   2 Sociable
Competitive 8   3 Need for Approval
Controlling 7   4 Dependent
6 Rigid   5 Tense

Stress and Your Personality

Your personality is the perceptual filter through which you experience the world and its potential stressors. For example, a person whose ACT Profile is characterized by high scores on the Tense, Rigid, and Controlling scales is the prototypical type A personality. Research indicates that type A people are hypervigilant. They experience high levels of stress in situations that are not stressful or are less stressful to other people.

The type A person is impatient, is quick to anger, and reacts with hostility to everyday occurrences like heavy traffic, waiting in a line, or not getting the service and attention expected. With constant stress and hostility as their norm, type A individuals are frequently in the fight or flight state, which causes wear and tear on the cardiovascular system, and consequently they do not live as long as other people.[6] Research using the Life Styles Inventory, which measures personality traits similar to those measured by the ACT Profile, shows strong relationships between personality and symptoms of stress. Their studies found that people with a personality profile dominated by counterproductive traits (Need for Approval, Dependent, Tense, Rigid, Controlling, Competitive) experience more stress-related medical symptoms than people with a personality profile dominated by the success traits.[7]

These aforementioned studies are consistent with the findings reported in a 1993 *Harvard Business Review* article that describes a study of the personality styles and behaviors that make Bell Labs engineers successful.[8] The study found that the most productive and valued engineers at Bell Labs were not those with the highest IQ or achievement test scores but those who excelled in teamwork, cooperation, and rapport. The engineers who formed alliances with other workers and used positive persuasion (versus authority or rank) and consensus building were the most successful. This study demonstrates how personality operates like a lens through which knowledge and skills are either sharpened or blurred.

All these research findings support the ideas promoted by the popular "emotional intelligence" school of thought[9] and the Big Five Model of Personality.[10] Emotional intelligence is typified by optimism, interpersonal sensitivity, positive persuasion, and conscientiousness (traits measured on the ACT Conscientious, Achieving, Innovative, and Helpfulness scales),

> The notion that brainpower does not equal organiza-tional horsepower is reflected in a study conducted by Michael Driver, a professor at the University of Southern California. The study found that students who scored highest on the Graduate Management Admissions Test (GMAT) were the worst equipped for real-world work. Driver looked at twelve hundred students that took the GMAT and completed a standard personality test and found that the students with the highest math scores lacked necessary social skills.

and has a greater impact on job performance than IQ, achievement test scores, or educational success. The Big Five Model of Personality is widely used for employee selection and development. The model measures five personality dimensions: conscientiousness, agreeableness, emotional stability, extroversion, and openness to new experiences. Research utilizing the Big Five finds that across professions, conscientiousness is the most consistent predictor of effectiveness. The conscientiousness dimension measures self-confidence, a sense

Rivets

When I was fourteen years old, I took my first flight, from Chicago to St. Louis on a small local airline. On the way to the airport, my dad briefed me on the new sensations and sounds I would experience: the landing gear being raised and lowered, the sound of the jet engines, the flaps, et cetera We arrived at the airport an hour early. Because I was a child traveling alone, I was allowed to pre-board the plane a half hour prior to departure. From my window seat, I gave the plane a careful inspection, looking to make sure that everything seemed in place. When I arrived in St. Louis, I called my dad. He said he'd been waving to me for the entire half hour while the plane sat at the gate in Chicago. "Why didn't you wave back?" he asked. I said I was too busy checking the rivets on the airplane wing just outside my window. I wanted to make sure they were all in place. As a kid on his first airline adventure, I figured that if the plane crashed it would be because one of the rivets that hold the plane together was missing. It wasn't until years later — as a psychologist on assignment to the airlines — that I realized that rivets don't hold an airplane together as much as the crew does.

of competence, organization, order, discipline, and the enjoyment of challenging work — essentially the same characteristics measured on the Conscientious and Achieving scales of the ACT Profile. Big Five studies also show that the attitudes and behaviors measured by the ACT Helpfulness and Sociable scales are linked with higher job performance.

Attitudes at Altitude: Lessons from Commercial Aviation

The first half of this chapter has focused on personality traits that are associated with high performance and those that are counterproductive and impede effectiveness and satisfaction in the workplace. We have also seen that there is a large body of research that demonstrates a clear relationship between personality and job performance across a wide range of professions. In the remaining half, I explore the role of personality in the performance of commercial airline pilots. I draw your attention to this specific example because in no other industry is the relationship between personality and performance on the job more dramatically and compellingly played out.

Seventy-five percent of commercial airline accidents are caused by human error, with flight crew failure at the top of the list. Three out of four plane crashes would not have occurred if the crew had practiced effective management and communications to resolve a critical situation. How do such lapses in basic leadership, management, and communications skills occur in this highly trained commercial airline pilot population? The former deputy head of flight safety at Swissair said, "We can change switches and instruments, but not human nature. We're all just 'normal' neurotics who must be taught to know and live with our problems and weaknesses."

Although human error is the leading cause of air accidents, it would be incorrect to conclude that the skies are filled with pilots who should not be flying. Pilots are an impressive group: intelligent, educated, and highly trained professionals who love their work more than any other professional group with which I've worked. They are dedicated to maintaining professional standards and bring a serious attitude to ongoing education and training. While it would be comforting to think of commercial airline pilots as infallible, pilots are human and make human errors. So when you review accidents where human error is the cause, remember it is easy to "Monday morning quarterback."

Transcript from the cockpit voice recorder as a plane is on its final approach for landing.

First Officer: Want me to fly today?
Captain: [*no response.*]
First Officer: What's the glide slope there, John?
Captain: Well, we know where we are ... we'll be alright.
Second Officer: Don't you worry, the fox is gonna have it wired.

(continued)

(continued)

First Officer: I hope so.

Captain: No problem.

First Officer: This a little faster than you normally fly this, John?

Captain: Oh yeah, but it's nice and smooth. We're gonna get in right on time, maybe a little ahead of time. We got it made.

First Officer: Sure hope so.

Second Officer: You know, John, what's the difference between a duck and a copilot?

Captain: What is that?

Second Officer: A duck can fly.

Captain: Well said.

First Officer: Seems like there's a bit of tail wind up here, John.

Captain: Yeah, we're savin' gas...help us get in a couple of minutes early too.

The airplane is now forty knots too fast and two hundred feet too low.

First Officer: John, you're just a little below the MDA [maximum descent altitude] here.

Captain: Yeah, we'll take care of it here.

First Officer: This is a little too high.

Captain: Yeah, gear down.

First Officer: You really look awfully high.

Captain: Fifteen degree flaps . . . twenty-five on the flaps.

First Officer: John, you're really high . . . you're gonna need forty on the flaps here to get this thing down. I don't think you're gonna make it, John, if you don't get this sucker on the ground.

Second Officer: Get it down, John.

First Officer: I don't think you're gonna make it. I don't think you're gonna make it.

Captain: We're going around. Oh darn.

Second Officer: 130, 140 knots.

First Officer: It isn't gonna stop, John. We're not gonna make it, John. Great job, John. I told you...jeez...

Sound of impact on cockpit voice recorder as the Alaska Airlines 727 crashes on landing at Anchorage Airport.

CREW RESOURCE MANAGEMENT TRAINING

FAA studies identify the seven most common flight crew failures as:

1. preoccupation with minor mechanical failures;
2. inadequate leadership;
3. failure to delegate tasks and to assign responsibilities;
4. failure to set priorities;
5. inadequate monitoring;
6. failure to use available data; and
7. failure to communicate intent and plan.

All these failures happen every day in every business. The common link? Personality and behavior styles. In commercial aviation, however, the consequences can be catastrophic.

Because human error (more often called "crew error" today) is the leading cause of airline accidents, the FAA requires that the airlines provide training to pilots in Crew Resource Management (CRM). Crew Resource Management is the effective use of equipment, crew members, ground-based personnel, and technical skills to achieve a safe and efficient flight operation. Every U.S. airline has a CRM course, sometimes referred to as "Captain's Charm School," that focuses on strengthening leadership, management, and communications skills. The objectives of CRM courses are to:

- enhance airline safety, efficiency, and morale through increased crew effectiveness;
- discuss and learn about behaviors that are effective or ineffective in flight operations; and
- help pilots learn more about their own leadership, management, and communications styles, compare their behavioral styles to the research on effective and ineffective CRM behaviors, and to make informed decisions on how to optimize their performance in a crew environment.

Most CRM courses include a discussion on *working with difficult crew members.* Here, pilots share stories that illustrate the interpersonal challenges that they face. During one CRM course, participants referred to a senior captain as "Rambo with stripes," and cited his infamous, aggressive, abrupt treatment of others and total lack of cooperation. His independent attitudes were so extreme that he was described as "thinking he's flying a single-seat piece of equipment." Since pilots bid for trips and are assigned them based on seniority, experienced pilots avoided bidding on trips they knew Rambo preferred. Thus, the pilots with the least experience flew with Rambo by default — creating a potentially dangerous situation where those who are perhaps the least capable of managing a difficult personality are nevertheless forced to do so.

Two Key Concepts in CRM: The Chain of Events and Situational Awareness

As in any business, airline accidents rarely occur because of one error. Accidents are the result of a series of situations and errors, a *chain of events.* This chain of events may be triggered by unforeseen problems that create unanticipated situations and distract the crew's attention from existing problems and from the primary task of safely flying the airplane. The flight crew's challenge is to maintain *situational awareness:* an accurate perception of the current conditions that affect the aircraft and the flight crew. A break in situational awareness occurs when a situation is misread or through a temporary lack of focus on the essentials of flying the plane. Strange as it may seem to non-pilots, the first rule of situational awareness is to ensure that someone is flying the airplane at all times.

This was the key lesson learned from Eastern Airlines flight 401. On December 29, 1972, the TriStar L1011 aircraft was making a typical nighttime approach to Miami in perfect weather when the crew put the wheels down. Indications were that the wheels had deployed but the landing gear indicator light did not go on. Apparently it had burned out. The captain was very explicit in directing the first officer and flight engineer in their attempts to fix the light. The crew's total preoccupation with the faulty light left no one with the singular responsibility to fly the plane, resulting in a loss of situational awareness. Unaware that the plane was losing altitude, the crew kept its focus on the landing gear light. Suddenly the first officer said, "Hey, our altitude can't be right; it says one hundred feet!" The crew unsuccessfully attempted to regain altitude. Ninety-nine people were killed when the plane crashed into the Everglades.

In addition to ensuring that someone is flying the plane at all times, other procedures are recommended to maintain situational awareness. Many of these procedures focus on assigning work and on rules for crew interactions that can help circumvent human error due to personality styles. Many of these methods apply to traditional work environments and can help to curtail human errors that arise from adverse interaction of personality styles on a work team:

- Never assume; always confirm
- Use all resources to gain information
- Give concise briefings about the status of operations
- Actively manage workload and distractions by delegating duties, verbalizing priorities, and acknowledging communications
- Use automation to reduce workload
- Actively manage alertness
- Ensure that tasks are accomplished in a timely manner
- Plan ahead — prepare for the next phase of the work
- Observe a sterile cockpit (talk about work-related matters, not stocks or sports)
- Actively monitor and be on the lookout for signs of reduced situational awareness
- Double-check critical information, not only from instruments but also from other team members

RESEARCH ON PERSONALITY AND FLIGHT CREW ERROR

Studies on flight crew effectiveness have been conducted since the mid-1980s by the Federal Aviation Administration

(FAA), the National Transportation Safety Board (NTSB), and the National Aeronautics and Space Administration (NASA).[11] Research has been conducted using flight simulators, during flights, and through the utilization of recordings from cockpit voice recorders recovered from accidents.

The results of these studies are stunningly consistent and have revealed that:

1. Crews led by captains with strong social skills and a high need for achievement make the fewest errors.
2. Crews led by captains with below-average achievement motivation and a negative expressive style (rigid and controlling) make more errors.

Studies at the Air Force Academy obtained similar results.[12] Flight crews led by captains who were controlling, focused only on tasks, and demeaned rather than encouraged others had the most errors. Captains who made the fewest errors showed the following behaviors:

- made use of all the available resources and delegated task responsibilities clearly
- communicated well with other crew members and established a cooperative tone
- established authority through competence rather than through rank
- encouraged others to be involved and provide input
- "walked the talk"

THE ACT PROFILE AND CREW EFFECTIVENESS

I have provided personality assessments and consulting services to the airlines for fifteen years, both in the United States and abroad. Airlines integrate assessments into CRM courses to help pilots understand their personality styles and to learn to better manage their behaviors in flight.

In the CRM courses we conduct an exercise in which we ask teams of pilots to create a profile of the "ideal" Crew Resource Manager. Team debates explore which personality traits are assets and which are negatives. Teams create an ACT Profile that reflects the personality style of an ideal Crew Resource Manager and that represents their benchmark for behavior excellence. More than fifteen hundred pilots have completed this profiling exercise, and there is agreement that behavior excellence is represented by high scores on the Conscientious, Achieving, Innovative, Helpfulness, and Sociable scales, as shown below:

Most-Effective Crewmember

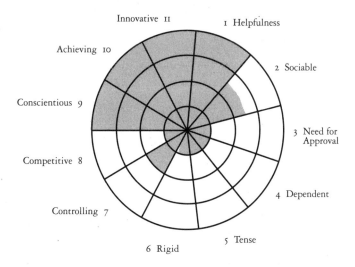

THE INTERACTION OF DOMINEERING AND DEFERENTIAL PERSONALITY STYLES

As mentioned, most accidents result from a chain of events that are often compounded by the interaction of a crew's ineffective behaviors. Rarely is an accident the direct result of a single crewmember; it is the combination of several personality styles that leads to flight crew failure, as the following example demonstrates.

Within the industry it is known simply as "Portland." It occurred in 1978 and is considered to be *the* accident that opened the eyes of the airlines to crew error as a major factor in accidents. United Airlines flight 173 ran out of fuel and crashed eight miles short of the Portland International Airport. The captain was a rigid, controlling person with poor listening skills. Unfortunately, he was matched with two deferring, nonconfrontational crewmembers. This combination of personality styles played out in a deadly fashion when the aircraft delayed landing because of a landing gear problem. The cockpit voice recordings indicate that the captain was totally focused on the emergency landing and preoccupied with the potential horrors of a crash rather than on appropriately delegating the many tasks associated with an emergency landing. Because he was so preoccupied, the captain didn't pay adequate attention to the fuel information his crewmates provided him. Several minutes after the flight engineer alerted him that the fuel level was low, saying, "You've got another two or three minutes," the captain responded, "Okay, we're going to go in now, we should be landing in about five minutes." The captain was surprised when the engines began to shut down eight miles and less than one minute away from the runway. Ten people were killed and twenty-three injured.

The NTSB determined that the entire crew had mismanaged the situation. The first and second officers did not communicate the urgency of the fuel situation or that an emergency landing was required immediately. The captain appeared oblivious to the critical shortage of fuel even though the other crewmembers warned him that only a few minutes of fuel remained. Soon after this accident, United Airlines began training pilots in crew coordination, leadership, and assertiveness, a program that continues today.

THE REAL "RIGHT STUFF"

One of the behavior patterns commercial pilots must overcome is the "right stuff" image: the strong, silent type who goes it alone and pushes the limits. What makes for success in the single-seat fighter pilot — considered the apex of flying — is exactly what undermines safety in a crew environment. The airlines have waged a battle against this misperception of the "right stuff," and most commercial airline pilots now understand that the behaviors that are required for leadership, management, and communications in the modern commercial cockpit are not those that make a fighter pilot great.

Perhaps no better example of this understanding exists than United Airlines Flight 232, July 19, 1989. Seventy-five minutes into the flight, the crew of this DC-10 was confronted with a mechanical problem that no one thought could happen.

The three-engine jumbo jet, under the command of Captain Al Haynes, departed Denver at 2:00 in the afternoon and climbed to a cruise altitude of 37,000 feet. At 3:15 P.M. the captain notified Air Traffic Control (ATC) that the number two engine had failed and that the airplane was "marginally controllable." The hydraulics system, essential to flying the plane, was not working. The plane rolled from 10-degrees left to 35-degrees right and experienced such severe vibrations that it was difficult to read the cockpit instruments. The passengers were informed of the engine failure and told to prepare for an emergency landing.

In the first-class cabin was Denny Fitch, a United Airlines training captain, and he immediately offered to assist the crew. Fitch recognized that the hydraulics were lost; he offered to try to manipulate the throttles to control the plane so other crewmembers could communicate with ATC and the United Airlines maintenance experts on the ground. Captain Haynes assumed the role of manager and leader and delegated the flying to the others.

Experts on the ground were unable to make any suggestions for flying the plane without hydraulic power, and ATC attempted to quickly locate the nearest airport that could accommodate a disabled jumbo jet. Sioux City was the best choice, although Haynes doubted the plane would make it to the airport. The calm teamwork and the inventiveness of the crew were all that was keeping the plane aloft. At one point Haynes and First Officer Al Records suggested that the throttles be cut. But Fitch said, "Nah, I can't pull 'em off or we'll lose it," and the captain deferred to Fitch's judgment.

As the damaged plane approached Sioux City, it was unstable, vibrating, and capable of making only right turns and very shallow left turns. During the final approach, Fitch, Records, and Haynes struggled to control the plane. Just prior to landing, the plane began to roll. Fitch applied extra power to try to control the plane, but the right wing hit the ground and the plane cartwheeled across the runway and burst into flames. Prompt action by the Sioux City Airport Rescue and Fire Fighting Unit saved many lives. Of the 284 passengers and crew, 184 miraculously survived.

Accident investigators determined that all passengers and crew would have been lost if the crew had not worked so effectively together. Captain Haynes retired shortly after the accident. He credited his training in CRM and the coordination skills of his fellow crewmembers for saving the 184 lives.

Conclusion

Examples from the airline industry dramatically demonstrate how personality styles can optimize or undermine performance in the cockpit. If your cockpit is a more traditional work environment, you can nonetheless learn from what is known about the real right stuff in pilots and apply those lessons to your own work. While the effects in your workplace may not be as dramatic, it nevertheless presents you with challenges that call upon you to muster all your abilities to lead, manage, and communicate with other team members in order for you to be successful.

Corporate folklore says that when you make your top salesperson the sales manager, you lose your best salesperson and the team gets a lousy manager. This bromide implies huge differences between personality characteristics that drive success in sales versus success in management. In fact, high performers are alike in more ways than they differ. They share a preference for demanding work that provides challenges; they are intellectually flexible and optimistic, and they are supportive and encouraging. The most successful salespeople *are* more competitive (and approval oriented) than high-performing managers. High-performing managers tend to be more conscientious than the most successful salespeople. But on balance, the personality traits that help make managers successful are the same traits that help make salespeople, executives, and commercial airline pilots effective.

In the following chapters, you will have many opportunities to apply the lessons you've learned about yourself and from the research on what makes or breaks performance in many different kinds of professions.

Notes

1. Peter Gratzinger, Ronald Warren, and Robert Cooke, "Psychological Orientation and Leadership: Thinking Styles That Differentiate between Effective and Ineffective Managers," in *Measures of Leadership,* ed. Kenneth Clark and Miriam Clark (Greensboro, N.C.: Center for Creative Leadership, 1990); Robert Kelley and Janet Caplan, "How Bell Labs Creates Star Performers," *Harvard Business Review* 71 (July–August 1993): 128–139; Robert Cooke and J. C. Lafferty, *Level 1: Life Styles Inventory, An Instrument for Assessing and Changing the Self-Concept of Organizational Members* (Plymouth, Mich.: Human Synergistics, 1982); Robert Cooke and Denise Rousseau, "The Factor Structure of Level 1: Life Styles Inventory," *Educational and Psychological Measurement* 43 (1983): 449–457; Robert Cooke and Denise Rousseau, "Relationship of Life Events and Personal Orientations to Symptoms of Strain," *Journal of Applied Psychology* 68, no. 3 (1983): 446–58; Robert Hogan and Joyce

Hogan, *Hogan Personality Inventory Manual,* 2d ed. (Tulsa, Okla.: Hogan Assessment Systems, 1995); Paul Costa and Robert McCrae, *Bibliography for the Revised NEO Personality Inventory* (NEO PI-R) and *NEO Five Factor Inventory* (Odessa, Fla.: Psychological Assessment Resources, 1994). Paul Costa and Robert McCrae, *Manual Supplement for the NEO 4* (Odessa, Fla.: Psychological Assessment Resources, 1994); Robert Baron and Gideon Markham, "Beyond Social Capital: How Social Skills Can Enhance Entrepreneurs' Success," *Academy of Management Executive* 14, no. 1 (2000): 106–15; Victor Dulewicz and Peter Herbert, "Predicting Advancement to Senior Management from Competencies and Personality Data: A Seven-Year Follow-Up Study," *British Academy of Management* 10 (1999): 13–22.

2. Gratzinger, Warren, and Cooke, "Psychological Orientation and Leadership: Thinking Styles That Differentiate between Effective and Ineffective Managers," (1990).

3. Cooke and Lafferty, *Level 1;* Cooke and Rousseau, "The Factor Structure of Level 1"; Cooke and Rousseau, "Relationship of Life Events and Personal Orientations to Symptoms of Strain."

4. Internal Study. Acumen International, Chris Guest, Ronald Warren, 1996.

5. Internal Study. Kenexa Technologies, Bob Bergman, Ronald Warren, 2001.

6. R. H. Rosenman, M. Friedman, et al., "A Predictive Study of Coronary Heart Disease," *Journal of the American Medical Association* 189 (1964): 15–22; Herbert Benson, *The Relaxation Response* (New York: Avon Books, 1975); Redford Williams, *The Trusting Heart* (New York: Times Books, 1989); Howard Friedman and S. Booth-Kewley, "The Disease-Prone Personality: A Meta-Analytic View of the Construct," *American Psychologist* 42, no. 42 (1987): 539–555.

7. Cooke and Rousseau, "Relationship of Life Events and Personal Orientations to Symptoms of Strain."

8   Kelley and Caplan, "How Bell Labs Creates Star Performers."

9. Daniel Goleman, *Emotional Intelligence* (New York: Bantam Books, 1995).

10. Hogan and Hogan, *Hogan Personality Inventory Manual;* Costa and McCrae, *Bibliography for the Revised NEO Personality Inventory and NEO Five Factor Inventory;* Costa and McCrae, *Manual Supplement for the NEO 4;* Edward Hoffman, *Psychological Testing at Work* (New York: McGraw-Hill, 2002).

11. T. Chidester, B. Kanki, H. C. Foushee, et al., *Personality Factors in Flight Operations, 1: Leader Characteristics and Crew Performance in*

Full-Mission Air Transport Simulation (NASA Technical Memorandum No. 102259, Moffett Field, Ames Research Center, 1990); T. Chidester, R. L. Helmreich, S. E. Gregorich, et al., "Pilot Personality and Crew Coordination: Implications for Training and Selection," *The International Journal of Aviation Psychology* 1, no. 1 (1991): 25–44; H. C. Foushee and R. L. Helmreich, "Cockpit Management Attitudes: Exploring the Attitude-Performance Linkage," *Aviation, Space and Environmental Medicine* 57 (1986): 1198–1200; H. C. Foushee and R. L. Helmreich, "Group Interaction and Flight Crew Performance," in *Human Factors in Aviation,* ed. E. L. Weiner and D. C. Nagel (San Diego, Calif.: Academic Press, 1988); S. E. Gregorich, R. L. Helmreich, and J. Wilhelm, "The Structure of Cockpit Management Attitudes," *Journal of Applied Psychology* 75, no. 6 (1990): 682–690; J. R. Hackman, "Group Level Issues in the Design and Training of Cockpit Crews," in *Cockpit Resource Management,* ed. H. W. Orlady and H. C. Foushee (NASA Conference Publication No. 2455, 1987), 23–29; R. L. Helmreich, "Cockpit Management Attitudes," *Human Factors* 26 (1984): 583–89; R. L. Helmreich and J. Wilhelm, "Determinants of Flight Crew Performance" (paper presented at the Human Factors seminar of the International Civil Aviation Organization, Leningrad, USSR, 1990).

12. R. Ginnett, "Behavioral Characteristics of Effective Crew Members," in *Proceedings of the Second Conference: Human Error Avoidance Techniques,* ed. (Moffett Field, Calif.: Ames Research Center, 1989); R. Ginnett, "First Encounters of the Close Kind: The First Meetings of Airline Flight Crews" (Ph.D. diss., Yale University, 1986); R. Ginnett, "Airline Cockpit Crew," in *Designing Effective Work Groups,* ed. P. S. Goodman (San Francisco: Jossey-Bass, 1986).

WHO YOU WANT TO BE

Have you ever taken time to think about how others perceive your work behavior? Do you think you have a good sense of how the people you work with would describe your behavioral assets and liabilities? Do you think others would create an ACT Profile that is similar or very different from your ACT Self-Profile?

If you were to create an ACT Profile that reflects how you would like to be in the future, what would it look like? Which of your traits and behaviors would remain like they are in your current self-profile and which would you modify, moderate, or develop?

In the preceding chapter you saw how effective or ineffective certain personality styles can be; in this chapter the focus is back squarely on you, and you will create two new ACT Profiles that reflect two important aspects of your personality: one profile will reflect how you think others perceive your behavior, and the other will reflect the attitudes and behaviors that you would like to have in the future.

These two new profiles will play an important role in your creation of an "action plan" for self-development in the concluding chapters.

Who do you think *they* think you are? How do you think the people you work with would describe you? Would they use such words as "conscientious" or "rigid" or "sociable" or "tense"? Would they say you are patient or abrupt? You are about to complete an ACT Profile that mirrors how you think others see you, your Mirror Profile. This exercise may seem simple, but to truly mirror the perspective of others requires real powers of empathy, honesty, and objectivity. Prepare yourself by thinking back to what others have said about your behavior. What have you heard in informal conversations or perhaps in a performance review that are clues to how others see you? What is your honest impression of how others experience your attitudes and actions?

After thinking this through, take a few minutes to carefully read all of the scale descriptions on the following page and consider how others would score you on each of the eleven assessment scales.

Once you have completed your Mirror Profile, take a few minutes to consider all that you've learned about personality and success, about yourself and your self-profile, and about how you think others perceive you. Then shift your attention to creating an ACT Profile to accurately reflect the kind of person you would like to be. Your self-profile is the image of the person you are now; this new profile will reflect the person you want to be. It is called your Character Profile.

The method you will use to complete your assessments for your Mirror and Character Profiles is different from the process you completed in your self-assessment. In the self-assessment you responded to sixty-four assessment items using a five-point scale to rate to what extent each item describes you. To complete your Mirror and Character Profiles, you will study the characteristics associated with each of the eleven ACT assessment scales and then mark on the profile the percentage that you think matches you. For example, in relation to your Mirror Profile, if you think others perceive you as trusting, patient, supportive, and encouraging, you will mark a high score on the Helpfulness scale. If you know that others see you as impatient, critical of others, and not providing them with much encouragement, you will mark a low score on this scale.

Organizations often hire me to deliver a "train the trainer" program to teach their internal training staff about personality assessments. I give an overview of the ACT Profile, describe the behaviors associated with the traits, and ask participants to identify famous people who typify each trait (e.g., Mr. Rogers, Helpfulness; Bill Clinton, Need for Approval; Woody Allen, Tense; Michael Jordan, Competitive; Albert Einstein, Innovative, et cetera). I then show the group another profile, which unbeknownst to them is mine, and ask them to talk about and interpret it. Participants enthusiastically provide interpretations such as:

- "This is a very independent person; someone who could not care less what other people think"
- "One tough cookie and someone who does not tolerate mistakes — a perfectionist"
- "Not very sociable. Self-absorbed. Focused on their own agenda"
- "An achiever...very intent on results and quality...a project person"
- "An egomaniac with an inferiority complex"

After the interpretations, I thank the group for their insights and tell them the profile is mine. Some people laugh and others are embarrassed by what they have said. I assure them that what they've said was fine, that I know I am imperfect and remain a work in progress.

About an hour later the participants receive their assessment results and the room becomes "you could hear a pin drop" silent. Inevitably, after reading their results, a few people will approach me and say, "You know, your assessment profile actually looks pretty good to me now."

Mirror Profile

To complete your Mirror Profile, read the descriptions of the eleven ACT personality traits and indicate on the scale how much of that trait you think others see in you. Remember that the profile has four concentric circles that correspond to the twenty-fifth, fiftieth, seventy-fifth, and hundredth percentile points, with the hundredth percentile at the outermost edge of the profile. If you believe that others would rate you as high on a trait, you will mark it above the seventieth percentile; average ranges from 35 percent to 70 percent; and low is below 35 percent.

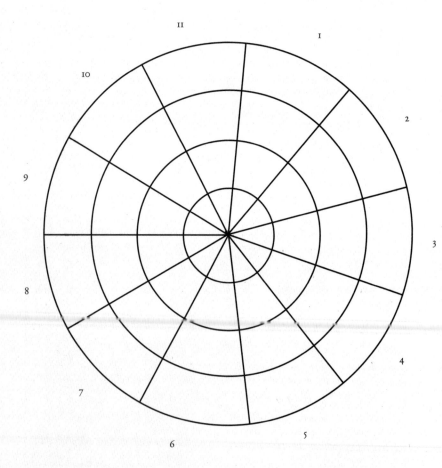

1. **Helpfulness:** trusting, patient, supportive, encouraging

2. **Sociable:** warmhearted, gregarious, friendly; loves to interact with others

3. **Need for Approval:** nonconfrontational; needs to be liked by others; very agreeable

4. **Dependent:** unassertive; prefers to follow; submissive

5. **Tense:** nervous, apprehensive, insecure; lacks self-confidence

6. **Rigid:** stubborn, inflexible, mistrustful

7. **Controlling:** bossy, aggressive, dominating; critical of others

8. **Competitive:** needs to win, brags about winning, makes everything a competition

9. **Conscientious:** disciplined, organized, careful, precise

10. **Achieving:** ambitious; likes challenges; enjoys work; likes to learn

11. **Innovative:** clever, confident, imaginative, creative

Now take a few minutes to honestly evaluate your Mirror Profile. Are there any surprises? Are there differences between your Mirror Profile and your Self-Profile? Do you think your coworkers would say that the Mirror Profile is a fair representation of how they perceive you? If you feel confident that it is a fair representation, move on; if not, make all necessary changes to the profile to create a more accurate picture of how you think they perceive you.

Who Are You?: An Assessment Story

In our first meeting, a future colleague, Tom, told me of his commitment to the sanctity of life. He said his appreciation extended to his willingness to pick up spiders and bugs that he found in the house and carry them outside, rather than to kill them. In spite of an obvious lack of spider empathy, I was invited to a party at Tom's home the following week. Relaxing on an outside deck, I noticed a row of electronic bug zappers

(continued)

Who Are You?: An Assessment Story (*continued*)

that appeared to be strategically placed to ensure a maximum kill zone on both the front and side patios. I was surprised and disappointed at this evidence of Tom's lack of authenticity and honesty. The person that Tom had said he was, was not what I observed. I sensed there might be other gaps between who this person claimed to be and who he really was.

Several months later, Tom participated in a 360-degree assessment. He was shocked by the feedback ratings from his coworkers. Tom's self-profile showed an assertive, conscientious, controlling, sensitive, and caring person. But his feedback profile showed an assertive, conscientious, controlling person who behaves toward others in an insensitive and uncaring manner. The feedback described a person who is overconfident of his own views and opinions and who will search for faults and shortcomings in those who disagree with him. Tom wanted to know, "How can it be that others don't see my true nature? How can this assessment be so wrong?"

Character Profile

To complete your Character Profile, read the descriptions of the eleven ACT personality traits and indicate on the scale how you would like to be. If you would like to be high on a trait, you will mark it above the seventieth percentile; average ranges from 35 percent to 70 percent; and low is below 35 percent.

1. **Helpfulness:** trusting, patient, supportive, encouraging
2. **Sociable:** warmhearted, gregarious, friendly; loves to interact with others
3. **Need for Approval:** nonconfrontational; needs to be liked by others; very agreeable
4. **Dependent:** unassertive; prefers to follow; submissive
5. **Tense:** nervous, apprehensive, insecure; lacks self-confidence
6. **Rigid:** stubborn, inflexible, mistrustful

7. **Controlling:** bossy, aggressive, dominating; critical of others

8. **Competitive:** needs to win, brags about winning, makes everything a competition

9. **Conscientious:** disciplined, organized, careful, precise

10. **Achieving:** ambitious; likes challenges; enjoys work; likes to learn

11. **Innovative:** clever, confident, imaginative, creative

Examine your Character Profile. Which scores on this profile are similar to those on your Self-Profile? What scores are different? On which assessment scales do you see the greatest differences between your Self-Profile and your Character Profile?

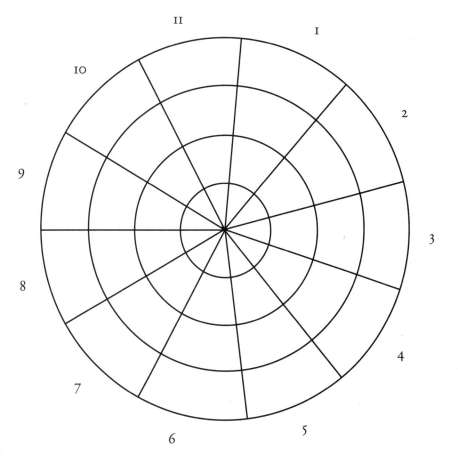

I worked on a study of several thousand mid-level managers who had completed a 360-degree assessment of sixteen management and leadership competencies. We compared self-ratings to coworker feedback ratings on skills such as planning, organizing, sharing information, empowerment, and teamwork. We discovered that one of every six professionals consistently overrates their skills, and conversely one of six consistently underrates skills. An "overrater" has self-ratings that are significantly higher than feedback ratings on 75 percent of the skills; an "underrater" has significantly lower self-ratings on 75 percent of the skills. Underraters tend to be modest about their competencies or lack self-confidence. Whatever the reason, it is a pleasure to see someone receive assessment results in which they are seen as more capable and talented than they feel. On the other hand, overraters tend to be arrogant and overestimate their skills.

What, if anything, surprised you? Do certain personality traits figure into your Character Profile either more or less prominently than you might have predicted prior to completing this exercise? What do these differences suggest about what you have learned about success and effectiveness? What do they suggest about what you have learned regarding the behaviors necessary to achieve your professional goals?

In the following chapters you will use your Mirror and Character Profiles to help you think through your personality assets and liabilities, to compare the kinds of work behaviors that you currently show to those that you would like to show to increase your job effectiveness. Having these two additional profiles provides you with needed perspective about yourself: how you see yourself (your ACT Self-Profile), how you think others see you (your Mirror Profile), and how you would like to see yourself (your Character Profile). You will compare all these perspectives with the research profiles from chapter 4 on the most and least effective professionals and begin to chart a pathway for behavior change that will increase your odds of becoming more successful and satisfied in your work.

c . h . a . p . t . e . r   6

RECOGNIZING AND WORKING THROUGH YOUR EMOTIONAL REACTIONS

These final four chapters will help you consolidate all the information about yourself and workplace effectiveness that you have created and read about in the previous chapters. You will compare your personal assessment results to the research on effective and ineffective work behaviors, and thus be able to make informed decisions on your goals and strategies for self-development. Armed with this information, you will create an action plan for behavior change and set a course for your future. Your goal is not to simply create an action plan but to incorporate changes to your everyday life. As Alfred North Whitehead said, "Ideas won't keep; something must be done about them."

This and the remaining three chapters are organized around a four-step behavior-change process originally introduced to me by Mark Brenner, founder of The Global Consulting Partnership™. Dr. Brenner has generously given permission to stretch and modify his behavior-change model for the purposes of this book, but the basic premise that you can think about change as a conscious, internally generated process comes from Dr. Brenner. In some circumstances this conscious process can be as easy as thinking before you act; in others, changes are more challenging to implement. The process has four steps that are briefly described below, and the first, Identify Your Emotional Reactions, is the focus of this chapter.

1. **Identify Your Emotional Reactions.** Understand that acknowledging a need for change is not an indictment of your character; it is a *sign* of character. The opportunity to change requires that you focus positively on improvements, not focus negatively on shortcomings. This is not always easy for people who have strong emotional reactions to their assessment data and become preoccupied with negatives rather than launching into ideas for solutions and improvements. The best way to begin is by working through your emotional reactions to your assessment results so that you can move from feeling vulnerable to feeling motivated to find constructive solutions.

2. **Complete a Reality Check.** When you compare your ACT Self-Profile to the research on effectiveness presented in chapter 4, you complete a reality check on your strengths and weaknesses. You can see, graphically, how your personality traits compare with those associated with high performance. You will also compare your ACT Self-Profile with your Mirror and Character Profiles that you created in the last chapter, working with all your assessment data so you can make informed decisions on behavior changes that you want to make. This is work you will complete in the next chapter.

3. **Develop an Action Plan.** Develop an action plan for change by choosing specific behaviors to start,

to stop, and to continue that will make you more successful and satisfied in your work. This is the focus of chapter 8.

4. **Commit Yourself.** Implementing your action plan requires your commitment to a conscious and disciplined effort. Success requires faith that even incremental changes yield significant benefits. You must maintain a positive attitude about your ability to implement your plan because whether you believe you can or can't do something, you are bound to be right.

Now, with a sense of where the final chapters of the book will take you, let's examine the topic of this chapter, understanding your emotional reactions to your ACT Profile.

Identify Your Emotional Reactions

My friend Ted completed an ACT Self-Profile and agreed it was "right on" and unsettlingly similar to feedback he'd recently received from his boss. His boss shared his impression that Ted is too aggressive and driven, does not take the time to carefully listen to others, gets frustrated, and reacts emotionally rather than rationally to people, events, and situations. Ted thought his boss was correct in his impressions but admitted "it makes me angry to no end that he thinks I'm not open-minded." Ted recognizes intellectually his deficits but, rather than listen to feedback and give it thoughtful, serious consideration, he becomes angry, and his anger prevents him from taking the next step of changing the behavior; he is not able to step back and allow his reason rather than his emotions to rule.

Many highly intelligent, motivated professionals likewise let their habitual emotional reactions get in the way of learning. Even some of us who say we relish constructive criticism can have strong emotional reactions when we receive negative feedback about our attitudes and behavior. It is easy to become defensive and shut out what others have to tell us, whether the feedback is delivered face-to-face or in a report.

Hard truths about our personality and behavior often generate emotions that block the impetus for change. Ted is a good example of that. We feel vulnerable when confronted by personal flaws or shortcomings and, in that state, some of us are unable to take a constructive approach to identifying the solutions that will make us more successful and satisfied. This may be especially true if the input or feedback you receive is surprising to you and you are taken aback. Think for a moment about your first reactions to your ACT Profile. Would you have felt comfortable immediately sharing it with your boss? Did you feel that it was information you needed to protect because it made you more vulnerable when it was there in black and white?

When you acknowledge the emotions generated by your ACT Profile, you have cleared a critical hurdle and are then ready to fashion a constructive response. To understand and sort out your emotional reactions to your assessment results, answer the following questions in Worksheet 1.

But before you do, I strongly recommend that you answer the questions, posed here and in the next three chapters, in a separate notebook or journal so that you will have ample room to note all your thoughts. It is important that you give yourself plenty of space to write out all your thoughts and feelings. A separate journal or notebook in which you have recorded your responses to these exercises will prove to be a beneficial tool for you to reflect on at a later date. Your answers may change over the years, and a complete record will show you where you were, how far you've come, and where you hope to be in the future.

Think about each question for a few moments before writing your answers in your journal or notebook. It is important that you actually write your responses, not just think about them in your head. Write your responses in pencil so that you can modify them if you want after you've reviewed them.

Worksheet 1 – Emotional Reactions to Your Profile

1. What caught your attention about your ACT Profile? Did you focus on your strengths, shortcomings, or a balance? Do you usually focus on positives or negatives?

2. How do you feel when you think about your personality traits that are ineffective? Do you feel disappointed, hurt, embarrassed, sad, worried, angry? Maybe you feel unconvinced and question whether the assessment is accurate, finding fault in something external to yourself rather than being fully willing to examine personal faults. Perhaps you feel no strong emotions. Whatever your feelings, write down all of your emotional reactions.

3. Do you have concerns that, by admitting your shortcomings, others will view you in the light of only your flaws, rather than as a fair mix of assets and liabilities?

4. Do your emotional reactions to your assessment results mimic how you react to feedback in general? For instance, if you were sad or angry about your assessment results, is that how you typically respond to unpleasant or bad news? How do you respond to bad news at work? With coworkers? At home? In your relationships?

5. Are you capable of accepting that you have personality shortcomings or flaws without diminishing the legitimacy of your assets and strengths?

You *must* work through your emotions in order to gain mastery of them. Use your emotional reactions to gauge your openness to new information. How willing are you to use feedback (from the assessment or from others) to uncover clues about new ways to be more effective rather than responding to feedback by defending behaviors that are counterproductive? My friend Ted, who reacts to things by getting "angry to no end," did not use his boss's feedback as an opportunity to develop self-control over his emotional reactions and learn from his uncomfortable experience. He merely repeated an old pattern, responded with his emotions, and, a few months later, lost his job. Rather than becoming angry and defensive in response to feedback, Ted would have benefited from understanding and accepting his shortcomings so he could rationally apply the lessons learned and chart a pathway to a more successful work experience.

Moving from Emotions to Constructive Problem-Solving

People commonly exhibit three emotional reactions to feedback that interfere with their ability to learn from it: rather than accept responsibility for our behavior, we often ignore, deny, or blame someone or something else. These defensive reactions are so second nature that you may not be aware you are responding defensively to feedback. But it is important to understand that any of these three emotional reactions will prevent you from learning from feedback and using constructive problem-solving methods to improve.

Each of these emotional reactions is described below, and while you read through the descriptions, think whether these emotional reactions play a role in your psychological defenses. Do you try to ignore feedback about areas you need to develop? Do you find that you would rather deny than confront issues in your life? Have others ever said to you that you find someone or something to blame rather than reflect on your role in problems or difficult situations? What events need to occur for you to move to acceptance of the validity of feedback about your developmental needs? What are the psychological mechanisms that have historically interfered with your ability both to accept full responsibility for your counterproductive behavior and to create the foundation to constructively solve how to change your behavior to be more effective at work?

IGNORE

Ignorance might be bliss for some matters, but when you are looking at your personality and behavior, ignorance is not bliss. Without insight into your attitudes and behaviors, you are stuck with unconsciously repeating them — whether they work well for you or not. Consider the differences between your ordinary work behaviors and how you might work on an important project or job assignment. When you are assigned important projects, you apply your intelligence, education, and experience and may consult with your peers to ensure the best possible outcome. You make a conscious effort to apply all your business smarts and technical knowledge to make sure the job is done right. Contrast this with your everyday approach to work. For most people, their work behaviors are more often the result of unconscious processes — habits — than of carefully crafted efforts. Illogical as it may be, people tend to ignore (or blame others for) past failures and problems and simply repeat what has not worked for them in the past.

People seldom apply their intelligence, education, experience, or a peer review process to their behavioral repertoire. It is the rare individual whose work behavior is the result of a methodical, thoughtful, critiqued effort. Because most people do not make conscious behavioral choices, they "default," or revert, to personality-driven habits, many of which are counterproductive.

Peter Ustinov said, "Once we are destined to live out our lives in the prison of our mind, our one duty is to furnish it well." This thought certainly can be applied to your behavior at work. Since you are destined to spend many, many hours in your place of work, it is in your best interests to perform well, to figure out what behaviors work and which do not and then apply that knowledge in your work life. That essentially is the task here: to understand your attitudes and behaviors, then choose to demonstrate those behaviors that help you to be more productive and satisfied at work and to learn to suppress those that are counterproductive. Easier said than done.

Unless a special effort is made to avoid it, you will lapse into old habits — especially in familiar situations like your workplace. Your job, if you wish to increase your ability to succeed and feel satisfied, is to gain control of counterproductive habits through sheer force of reason and will, through a conscious, disciplined effort to change your behavior (for those of you who cannot handle the concept of *change,* because it just feels TOO BIG, try expressions like *modify* or *moderate* instead of the word *change*). Changing your behavior requires that you think about how your personality traits affect the way you communicate, collaborate, set goals, deal with conflict, and feel about things. These issues are complex, but be reassured that even slight behavior modifications can mean the difference between success and failure. And remember: ignoring problems will ultimately be more painful than finding the solution to them

DENY

Denial takes two forms. The first is to refute the validity of the feedback on your behavior and the second is to accept the validity of the feedback but refute that in your case the behavior is counterproductive. According to the first type of denial, a person might say, "I don't think I'm pushy," and, following the second type, someone might say, "I'm pushy, but that's the only way to get anything done around here."

In relation to denying the validity of feedback, I find it interesting that in the context of the ACT Profile, people rarely reject all their results; instead, I've found that people will accept the accuracy of the results around their strengths but (some) disagree with the description of their counterproductive behaviors. As a pilot I worked with said, "I looked at my strengths and, yeah, that's me. Then I saw those weaknesses or my behavior shortcomings, and I thought, now wait a minute, I'm not like that. . . . Of course, much later I came around to understanding that the strengths and short-comings were both a pretty accurate rendering of me."

Another person I worked with said, "I'm just not sure that I buy into this description that I am so competitive. I don't think I am." I responded, "Okay. That may be true. How do you feel about the accuracy of the rest of the report? Are there other strengths and weaknesses that you think de-scribe you?" Her response was, "Yes, most of this is definite-ly me. But I don't agree that I am as competitive as this report says."

If you feel that part of the assessment is accurate and part is not, for the moment put aside your concerns about what doesn't seem accurate. If, for instance, you are like my friend and you don't think you are competitive, put it aside for the moment. Work with those strengths and counterproductive tendencies that resonate with you, but rather than simply discarding the feedback about the other parts, ask three or four people who know you well if they think you are com-petitive, or tense, or pushy, et cetera. If they do not see you as particularly competitive, or tense, or pushy, et cetera, put that issue aside. However, if they tell you that you have any of these traits, put competitiveness at the top of your list for self-development, because you are in denial that it plays a significant role in your behavior.

The second form of denial is to agree that counterproductive traits are prominent in your personality makeup but deny that they have a negative impact on your performance. This is common among people who have attained some success as a result of their intelligence and technical skills. Their history of success makes it easier to discount the importance of their personality traits in their human-capital equation. For instance, very aggressive, pushy people may excuse their always-on-the-offense style by saying, "that's what got me where I am today," thinking they are commenting on their success, when in fact their intelligence and hard work is what brought *some* success while their hostility likely brought them high blood pressure and bad relationships.

A sure sign of a healthy ego is the ability to put the "best possible spin" on bad news. Confronted with assessment results that show the need to change, some of us are tempted to hide behind our old friend, denial. It can be intoxicating to conclude that we are "the exception to the rule" or "that life has worked out pretty well so far." But that intoxication begs a critical question: have you attained your level of success because of or in spite of your personality and its impact on your work behavior?

If this second form of denial is familiar to you, ask

A Story about Denial

A recent survey reported in the *Journal of the American Medical Association* found that a majority of cigarette smokers do not believe they run a higher-than-average risk of heart disease or cancer. Despite decades of publicity shouting the results of research that clearly identifies smoking cigarettes as a serious threat to health, astoundingly, only 29 percent of smokers believed they had a higher-than-average risk of heart attack and only 40 percent believed they were at greater risk for cancer! What is truly amazing is that most of these people would agree that the research is valid and that cigarettes do pose a real health threat for most people, but that this research does not specifically apply to them.

yourself what has led you to evaluate your strengths and weaknesses at this particular time. You have committed significant time and effort to complete the assessments and to read the previous chapters in this book. You have progressed to a point in this book where you will soon need to objectively evaluate your strengths and counterproductive styles in order to complete your action plan. You have already progressed a long way in terms of building the knowledge required to become the person you want to be. Now I urge you to continue your quest to optimize the "human" in your human capital and enjoy the fruits of your labors.

BLAME

Blame is expressed in three familiar forms: self-blame, blame of others, and blame on outside influences in the world.

Self-blame, guilt, is a very popular form. It does no good to feel guilty about your personality and behavior styles unless this awareness leads to change. Guilt alone has no benefit, so if you feel compelled to take a dip in the pool of self-pity, make it brief. While it is important and constructive to be aware of your flaws and shortcomings, becoming preoccupied with them serves no useful purpose and is in fact destructive. Many people focus too much on their negative attributes and feel diminished by the presence of any counterproductive traits; what is most beneficial, however, is to maintain a balanced perspective on both strengths and weaknesses. Perfection is an unattainable ideal, but improvement is possible. Accept that you are imperfect and get on with it.

The second form of blame is the often used, frequently abused, blame of others. Perhaps because 75 percent of your coworkers have counterproductive personality styles, it is easy to see them as prime targets for blame. The fact that 75 percent of workers have personality problems that they carry with them to work means a stressful work environment, and under stressful conditions some people place blame on others. However, you must gently remind yourself that blame doesn't solve the problem, it only displaces it. Besides, I know of very few people who can actually have an impact on changing a coworker's personality or behavior. But, you can certainly change your own. When you master your own behavior, your relationships with others will improve and perhaps your more positive interactions will serve as an impetus for coworkers to make improvements as well.

The final form of blame is the familiar tendency to blame outside influences in the world for problems. Your work situation, company politics, family stress, the economy — these are just a few outside influences that are common targets of blame. Often there *are* truly legitimate issues, problems, and irritations that the external world generates. But, your goal is not to change the external world — an impossible task — but to master your own attitudes and behaviors in the world in which you must operate effectively. One key to more successfully negotiating your way in a stressful world is for you to understand how you respond to stress and then to change or moderate your responses to better cope in a stressful world.

Moving from Defensiveness to Acceptance

Which of the emotional and defensive reactions described above resonate with your personal experience? Were any of them familiar to you? Take a few moments and review your responses to Worksheet 1 that you completed earlier in this chapter. With the descriptions of deny, ignore, and blame fresh in mind, reread your responses and make changes as necessary. Also, add your response to the following question: What form of defensive reaction do you show when confronted by your shortcomings and flaws? Do you use denial? Ignore the feedback? Blame someone or something? Or, do you respond with an open mind and accept the feedback as information to learn from, as knowledge that motivates your self-development and growth?

Acceptance

What is required of you to accept and use the information in this book to promote your self-development and growth? What you must have in order to comfortably move forward and accept a need to change your behavior is faith in three tenets of this book. First, belief that the research presented here showing distinct relationships between personality traits and on-the-job effectiveness is valid. Second, that personality traits and behaviors (usually) operate like habits, without conscious control, and by exerting conscious control, you can modify your behaviors at work. Third, that your personality has an impact on your job effectiveness and that by taking control of how you act, you can increase your effectiveness and satisfaction on the job.

A Pilot Learns to Speak Up

Lyle is an example of an individual who took his assessment results to heart, constructed an action plan, and changed his behavior. Lyle is a commercial airline pilot, a first officer who is second in command to the captain. Lyle has ten years of commercial flying experience and is enthusiastic, bright, capable, socially skilled, but reticent to speak up when in the company of more experienced and assertive crew members. Lyle participated in one of the first Crew Resource Management training sessions I conducted. He had sought me out for assistance on several occasions and shared with me the assessment results identifying a need to be more assertive, particularly in a situation where he felt the safety of the flight was in question. Lyle had not been aware of the research that indicated that accidents were sometimes the result of a crew member not speaking up; he'd assumed that it was overaggressive, dominating captains, who "made others too uncomfortable to speak," that were the cause of communication breakdowns that led to accidents. Lyle learned it was his obligation to speak up if he disagreed with a captain, regardless of his lesser experience or his personal discomfort with conflict. Lyle made assertiveness the focus of his action plan.

(continued)

A Pilot Learns to Speak Up (*continued*)

Several months after our training sessions, I ran into Lyle, and he told me that he'd put his assessment results to good use, perhaps avoiding an accident. He was on a flight with a crew that was stressed and tired because they were flying a late-night route and had been delayed for over four hours by bad weather and mechanical problems. Everyone was exhausted and touchier than usual. Except for communications about flight status, they'd flown in silence for two hours. On final approach to land, Lyle was not comfortable with the speed and altitude of the plane. But the captain was flying and Lyle was reluctant to voice his questions and concerns. However, his commitment to what he'd learned in Crew Resource Management required he speak up and not allow his personality style to get in the way of doing his job right. So Lyle said, "I'm not comfortable with this approach. We're a little high and fast. . . . What do you think?" To his surprise, the captain gave his immediate agreement: "You're right. Thanks for saying something. I am totally beat. Let's do a go-around and try this again." Lyle told me he was unsure if their initial landing attempt would have had problems, but he knew he did the right thing. He laughed at his assumption that the captain would "jump down my throat" — and how that false assumption would have prevented him from speaking up in the past. The captain had welcomed his input and Lyle was sure that he'd continue being more assertive in the future.

BELIEF 1

You must have (some) faith that the research described in the previous chapters is valid and meaningful for you. The studies show that there are many ways to be ineffective or dysfunctional at work, but more important, they also identify ways to be more effective and functional and thus more satisfied in the workplace. It is necessary that you believe that, using the research studies as a guide and your ACT Self-Profile and Mirror and Character Profiles as important personal data tools, you can chart a path to greater effectiveness.

The idea that there is a more optimal personality profile

than what a person now has may be difficult for some people to accept. For some the idea may raise the specter of "cloned behavior." Some might fear there is a risk of losing those special values, beliefs, and qualities that make them unique. Nevertheless, such doubts and fears can be put aside; you can modify those attitudes and behaviors that get in the way of satisfaction and effectiveness in the workplace and still maintain your individual liberties, freedom of expression, and diversity.

Indeed, although you are more than your behavioral style at work, the role of personality and its impact on your work experiences and behavior are important, yet often overlooked. Your personality drives pervasive habits that are at the root of the way you communicate, collaborate, set goals, and deal with conflict. And like many habits, personality-driven work styles are habits that you either break or they will break you. Why? Because, as noted earlier in this book, your personality is a conduit through which the expression of all your other forms of human capital flow — your IQ, education, job knowledge and skills, and experience. Consequently, your

Graceful Acceptance

I was giving a seminar on the role of personality to a group of very bright management consultants. These were great people to work with because they had the confidence, intellect, and experience to allow them to view their personality shortcomings without becoming defensive or feeling devastated. One fellow in particular was wonderful. At the point in the seminar where participants had the opportunity to share with the others what they had learned about their personality and its impact on their consulting ability, this fellow said, "Well, this assessment is right on. It says I am dogmatic, opinionated, abrupt, self-absorbed, aggressive, and forceful. And those are my strengths!" His comments set the tone for a fun and comfortable learning environment where everyone could more easily accept their imperfections and then spend their precious energy working to improve their work styles.

goal should be to gain enough insight into your specific personality predispositions and learn to moderate or modulate your personality style in order to facilitate rather than restrict the flow of your human capital. And again, this does not mean a total makeover of all the different values, interests, and ways of looking at the world that make you uniquely you; it means becoming aware of and changing those parts of yourself that get in the way of getting the most out of your working life.

BELIEF 2

You must also believe that personality traits and behaviors are like unconscious habits, and that it is possible to consciously modify your behavior in the workplace. Most people today know that the only way an alcoholic, drug addict, or gambler can overcome their addiction is to acknowledge the addiction and then accept full responsibility to consciously monitor and change the behavior around that addiction.

Similarly, people with counterproductive work behaviors can change only when they make a conscious, disciplined effort to monitor and alter counterproductive habits. So, while you may be predisposed to act in a particular way (to give in to your habit), you have the free will to choose how to act (to not give in to your habit). The good news is that if you choose to exercise your free will and make the effort to master a habit, you can succeed.

BELIEF 3

Finally, you must believe that your personality has an impact on your effectiveness at work and that by taking control of your behavior, you can increase your effectiveness and satisfaction on the job.

Moving to Solutions

Now that you have worked through the initial emotional responses to your profile and accept that some changes can increase your effectiveness, it's time to apply yourself to solving the problems. I refer to this as the problem-solving stage because you need to actively seek solutions to change situations that, without your intervention, will persist, remain problematic, or prevent you from being as successful or satisfied as you can be. In order to uncover good solutions, you need to have a solid sense of where you are now and where you want to be in the future. You need to do a reality check.

This reality check is exactly what you will do in the following chapter. The logical place to start is to evaluate your current work situation and examine your job challenges, stresses, and opportunities. Then, building upon your Mirror Profile, you will predict how coworkers might describe your strengths and limitations — predictions that you will confirm or disconfirm in discussions you'll have with them prior to creating your action plan. Finally, in chapter 8, you will apply all your knowledge about your own attitudes and behaviors and the research on effective and ineffective behaviors to identify specific development opportunities around which you will build your action plan.

c . h . a . p . t . e . r   7

WORKING WITH YOUR ACT SELF-PROFILE

I n the last chapter you were introduced to a behavior-
change model and explored three common types of emotional reactions that interfere with solving problems.
Many people ignore, deny, or place blame on other people or
conditions in the world in order to protect themselves from
having to confront personal shortcomings. When faced with
personal liabilities, it is easy to get defensive and resist examining seriously the need to change. In the long run, facing
and dealing with counterproductive behaviors will prove to
be far more effective for you than persisting in demonstrating behaviors that get in the way of your success and satisfaction.

This chapter calls upon you to confront work situations
that are stressful and challenging for you and answer some
tough questions about your strengths and weaknesses. You will
be invited to think of new ways to more effectively manage
your work life, and you will be given methods for soliciting

input and feedback from your coworkers to help you learn more about how others at work experience you.

This chapter is the most demanding chapter in the book because you will be asked to:

- answer a series of questions to help you evaluate and reflect on your current work situation;
- predict how others would describe your strengths and limitations and compare your predictions with your Mirror Profile, making any necessary modifications;
- compare your ACT Self-Profile with your Mirror and Character Profiles;
- compare your ACT Self-Profile with the research profiles on the most and least effective professionals; and
- evaluate all the information so you can begin to make informed and conscious choices for the future you want to create for yourself.

These exercises will help you understand how personality-driven behaviors are played out in your life at work. They will help you uncover and accurately define the self-generated barriers that get in the way of your achieving greater success and satisfaction. By the end of this chapter, you will have the data that you need to begin to chart a course to a better future for yourself at work.

Let's begin then with your current work situation.

> If you are dissatisfied with your work situation but cannot, by the end of this chapter, think of things you can change, turn to your network of coworkers, friends, and family for their perspectives and advice. This will provide you with a great opportunity to listen to others and see things from a different point of view.

Worksheet 2: How You See Your Work Situation

1. What do you want to accomplish in your career?

2. What do you want to accomplish in your current job?

3. What are your most interesting challenges at work?

4. What do you see as your best opportunities in your current work?

5. What do you think are your biggest problems at work?

6. What are your behavioral strengths that help you succeed in your career?

7. What are your behavioral limitations that hold you back from advancing in your job or your career?

8. What kinds of situations create stresses for you at work?

9. How do you know when you are experiencing stress? What do you feel? How do you behave?

10. If you could change just one thing in your work environment to make work more pleasant for you, what would that change be?

11. If you could change just one thing about your attitude toward work that would make your work more pleasant for you, what would that change be?

Review your answers.

- Evaluate your responses carefully to see if there are things that you want to add or change.
- Do new ideas or insights come to mind upon review?
- Make note of factors and influences that you can realistically change about your work situation and notice which factors are beyond your control. It is essential to identify the things that you can change in your work situation and not spend precious time on things that you cannot alter. If this is difficult for you to do, put it aside and complete this exercise later. You may find that completing the next series of questions, on how coworkers would describe your behavior, will provide you with additional clues about your current work situation.

How Coworkers Would Describe Your Behavior

What would your coworkers say are your behavioral strengths? Do you consider these behaviors as positives or negatives? What would your coworkers describe as your limitations? Do you consider these limitations as positives or negatives? For example, you may see your willingness to get pushy and forceful in order to get what you want as positive — you are willing to fight for what you think is important. You may view this behavior as appropriate assertiveness and as a key asset. Coworkers may view this same behavior as a significant limitation and as a negative, counterproductive behavior. They may well view it as inappropriate bossiness and counterproductive to the concept of teamwork.

Oftentimes people get new insights into their behavior by attempting to look at it from the point of view of others. That was part of what you did in constructing your Mirror Profile. In that exercise you focused on how you think others see your personality profile; the following questions ask you to explicitly define what others would say are your strengths, weaknesses, and development needs. Take your time in responding to the following questions, doing your very best to answer as you think others would describe your behavior. Be very careful not to respond based upon how you might *want* them to describe your behavior; honestly and accurately describe how you think coworkers see your behavior.

Worksheet 3 – How Coworkers Would Describe Your Behavior

1. What would coworkers say are your behavioral strengths that help you succeed in your career? Do you consider these behaviors positive or negative and why?

2. What would coworkers describe as your behavioral limitations that hold you back from advancing in your job or your career? Do you consider these behaviors positive or negative, and why?

3. How would others describe your behavior when you are experiencing stress?

4. What would your coworkers say are your biggest problems at work?

5. If your coworkers were asked what one change in your behavior would make you more effective at work, what would they say?

Compare your responses to these questions with your responses to the first set of questions about your work situation in Worksheet 2. Where do the responses overlap and where are they different? If there are differences, what accounts for these differences between your self-perceptions and how you think others perceive your personality at work? Is there agreement about what behaviors are strengths and which are limitations? What do these two sets of responses indicate about your behavior in your current work situation and what do they suggest about behaviors that you might want to change?

How do your responses to the questions of how coworkers would describe your behavior agree with or conflict with the behaviors reflected in your Mirror Profile? Take a few minutes to compare and contrast these two sets of information about how you think others perceive you. After comparing your written responses with your Mirror Profile, if there are any changes you would like to make to your Mirror Profile, make them now.

Examining Your Self-Profile

In this section you will compare your ACT Self-Profile with the profiles of the most and least effective professionals, with your Mirror Profile, and with your Character Profile. The purpose of these exercises is to help you gain perspective on your current attitudes and behaviors and to begin thinking about the kinds of behaviors you want to start, stop, and continue, which will be the core of your action plan.

The first step in this examination is to compare your ACT Self-Profile and your Mirror Profile that you created in chapter 5.

Just as there are often large differences between self-assessment results and 360-degree ratings (where others rate your behavior), there are often differences between a person's ACT Self-Profile and their ratings on their Mirror Profile.

Many of us are perceived differently than we see ourselves and some of us have a good sense of how others perceive us without even collecting 360-degree ratings.

When answering the following questions and comparing your ACT Self-Profile and Mirror Profile, look for consistencies and differences. Keep an open mind and watch for new information, things you may not have noticed before.

The following worksheet will ask you to identify specific behaviors to start, stop, and continue in order to be more effective or satisfied on the job.

- Behaviors that you start are those you currently do not exhibit. For example, an unassertive person might start asking more questions. A person who acquiesces too easily might start taking a firmer stand on important issues. Someone who gets into heated arguments might start asking for a time-out when things move from friendly disagreement to conflict.

- Behaviors that you stop are ones you currently show but would like to not display in the future. For example, an individual who constantly criticizes what others say or do might choose to not comment. A person who feels compelled to always say yes and volunteer for more work than is feasible might stop saying yes and set reasonable limits.

- Behaviors that you continue are existing strengths that you will make a conscious effort to use even more in the future.

Worksheet 4: Self-Profile and Mirror Profile

1. In what ways is your ACT Self-Profile similar to your Mirror Profile?

2. In what ways is your ACT Self-Profile different from your Mirror Profile? Go around the entire profile and note where there is a significant difference, of at least 25 percent between the two profiles. Where there are significant differences, consider how these differences get played out in your behavior on the job.

3. Now, considering these similarities and differences, what do they suggest about behaviors that you can start, stop, and continue in order to be more effective in your current work environment? Think of specific behaviors that you can start, stop, and continue that are good candidates to include in your action plan. For example, if you think others see you as more helpful than you see yourself, this behavior would be a good candidate to continue in your action plan. If you think others see you as more rigid, this is a good candidate for a behavior that you may want to stop in your action plan. Write down your observations. If you are unsure which assessment scales are associated with effectiveness or a lack of effectiveness and thus represent behaviors to start or stop, go back to chapter 3 and reread the scale descriptions.

Worksheet 5: Self-Profile and Research Profiles

Next, review and compare your ACT Self-Profile with the Research Profiles of the most- and least-effective professionals (in chapter 4). Look for patterns that illustrate your potential strengths and weaknesses and clues for behaviors to start, stop, and continue in order to increase your effectiveness and satisfaction in your work. Write down your answers to the following questions:

1. In what ways is your ACT Self-Profile similar to the Research Profiles of the most-effective professionals? Don't look for differences, only commonalities.

2. The most-effective profiles have high scores on Conscientious, Achieving, Innovative, Helpfulness, and Sociable. Are any of your highest scores on these traits? If so, the behaviors that reflect these traits are strong candidates to include in your action plan as behaviors to continue at work. If none of these traits is prominent for you, the behaviors associated with these traits are good candidates to include in your action plan as behaviors to start at work.

3. Based on this comparison between your ACT Self-Profile and the profiles of the most effective professionals, describe one or two behavior changes that, if implemented, would make you more effective in your work.

4. Compare your ACT Self-Profile to the Research Profiles of less-effective professionals. Does your self-profile have any of the traits of less-effective professionals? Do you have relatively high scores on the Need for Approval, Dependent, Tense, Rigid, Controlling, or Competitive scales? If so, which ones are the most prominent in your ACT Self-Profile? How do these particular traits currently drive behaviors that get in the way of your being more effective and satisfied in your work situation?

(continued)

Worksheet 5 (*continued*)

5. In comparing your ACT Self-Profile to the profiles of less-effective professionals, does your profile suggest behaviors that you would want to start, stop, and continue at work? For instance, a high score on Dependent may suggest to you that if you stop being as dependent on others as you are, you would feel more satisfied with yourself, perhaps raising your self-esteem and your productivity. Or, a high score on Controlling may suggest to you that if you allowed yourself to listen more carefully to input from others, your interpersonal relationships and job performance might improve. Write out your observations.

6. Based on this comparison between your ACT Self-Profile and the profiles of the less-effective professionals, describe one or two behavior changes that, if implemented, would make you more effective in your work.

7. Finally, compare your ACT Self-Profile with your Character Profile, which, you'll recall, reflects the type of person you want to be. What behaviors would you need to start, stop, and continue in order to move from where you currently are to where you want to be?

You now have a large database of information about yourself that you can ponder and work with:

- How does the information you've derived from this exercise jibe with what you have heard others say about you in the past — in arguments, in peer reviews, in performance reviews, in casual talks at work and at home?
- Given your current work situation, what behaviors can you start or stop that would minimize self-generated barriers to satisfaction or productivity?
- What behavior changes would lead you to feel more satisfied about who you are and what you do at work?
- Given your current work situation, what behaviors would your coworkers say are most ripe for change? What behaviors would they suggest you start or stop to increase your success and satisfaction?

You have realized the goal of this chapter when you are prepared to have a conversation with your coworkers about how you behave at work. Their impressions of which of your personality traits can be leveraged for greater success and satisfaction and which drive behaviors that get in your way at work will help you confirm or modify your conclusions from the previous exercises in this chapter.

What to Do If You Can't Get a Clear Picture of Your Behavioral Assets and Liabilities

Most people can identify changes they would like to make in order to be more effective and satisfied in their work situation, but if you cannot think of any behavior changes — and it does happen — that will help you to become more productive and satisfied at work, ask your coworkers for feedback about your work behavior (see "Soliciting Input from Coworkers"). After talking with your coworkers, repeat the Mirror Profile exercise and then complete or revise your responses to the questions in this chapter based upon your conversations with coworkers.

Soliciting Input from Coworkers

The final exercise of this chapter is for you to seek input from those who are familiar with your behavior at work. The goal here is to talk with three or four of your coworkers and to develop a clear understanding of how others see your behavioral strengths and limitations. This might sound like an uncomfortable situation to put yourself in, but if you follow the suggestions listed below and prepare well, this will be a very positive and information-rich experience.

Here's a script that describes one way to ask your coworkers for their input:

I've just completed a set of personality and behavior assessments that have made me more aware of my personal assets and liabilities. I've already put a lot of work into this effort and I am committed to developing new skills and behaviors that will allow me to become more effective here at work.

Part of my self-development effort includes collecting input from people who are familiar with my work behavior. I would appreciate it if you'd share your perceptions of my strengths and weaknesses. I am most interested in understanding how my behavior either helps or gets in the way of my performing at a higher level on the job. This might include how I set goals, achieve results, work with others, and any observations and suggestions you have for how I can work more effectively with you and others on the job.

In particular, I am interested in learning about any behaviors that you think would be to my benefit to start, stop, and continue here at work. For instance, from the assessments and study that I've already completed, I think I could be more effective if I were to _____. (Fill in the blank with an example of a behavior that you consider a good candidate to start or stop — for example, start listening better; start asking more questions; start taking more risks; stop raising my voice; stop taking on more work than I know I can complete on time; stop criticizing others; et cetera)

(continued)

> **(continued)**
>
> If you are comfortable with the idea, I would appreciate it if you could find a thirty- or forty-five-minute time slot to talk with me about your impressions and recommendations. I value your input, will listen carefully to what you have to say, and hope you can help me out with this.

If your coworker is comfortable with a face-to-face discussion scenario, set a time and thank them. If they would rather not meet, express your appreciation for their consideration and suggest that "if you would be comfortable, perhaps you could anonymously write down your observations and suggestions, like some other coworkers might do."

PREPARING FOR YOUR CONVERSATION

Following are a few guidelines to prepare you for a productive conversation with your coworkers about your work behavior. First, be pleasant, maintain an open mind, and avoid reacting defensively to anything that is said in the meeting. Review your responses to the exercise questions in this chapter and be particularly sensitive to any interpersonal or communication issues that could influence your ability to follow these guidelines in your upcoming conversation. For example,

- if your self-assessment results indicate that you talk more than listen, pre-pare yourself to listen, to not interrupt, and to limit your talking to asking open-ended questions that will help your coworker tell you more about their impressions;
- if your tendency is to be unassertive and to avoid asking tough questions, be sure to prepare and use a list of questions to serve as a discussion guide for your meeting. You can use the list of suggested questions on the following page to help you get started. Be sure to also write down follow-up queries to ensure you get details and examples that will make it absolutely clear to you what your

coworker's impressions of your behavior styles are. Practice asking tough questions in a tactful way. Prior to meeting with your coworker, practice asking your list of questions and follow-up queries with a friend or significant other so you are familiar and comfortable with the discussion format; or

• if you tend to be argumentative, prepare yourself to support and encourage your coworker on their feedback, regardless whether you agree with their perspective or not. Use active listening, ask open-ended questions, and employ paraphrasing techniques ("if I understand you correctly, you are saying that I don't take enough time with others on the team and that I get impatient") to facilitate communication. Under no conditions are you to argue with the person giving you their impressions and feedback. Remember, your goal in this exercise is to fully understand their point of view, not convince them that you know better.

> If you are uncomfortable with a face-to-face discussion with colleagues of your strengths and weaknesses, you can ask your coworkers to anonymously write down their observations and suggestions. If you choose this option, create a worksheet to give to your coworkers to make their job easier and to guide their feedback. Create this worksheet by summarizing the questions that are recommended for the face-to-face discussion format below.

Suggested Questions to Ask Coworkers

The following list provides suggestions on how to conduct the discussion, the kinds of questions to ask, and different ways to ask questions about your behavioral assets and liabilities. Do not ask all these questions; select those that feel right to you and add others if necessary to create your own list of questions that you want to be sure to ask in your conversation.

- Since it is often easier to begin with strengths or assets, you may want to start by asking your coworker to describe what they see as your behavioral strengths that are helping you succeed on the job. What do you do well? What kinds of personal and interpersonal behaviors have they seen you excel at? Ask them to provide an example of when you demonstrated that specific behavior and why they thought you were particularly effective.

- What are the types of situations that they see as creating stress for you? What behaviors have they observed in you when you are stressed? What suggestions can they provide to help you avoid stressful situations or for coping with the stress more effectively?

- What are your coworker's impressions of your behavioral shortcomings and limitations that get in your way of higher performance? Can your coworker describe a time when your performance on the job disappointed them, where they expected better of you? Can they provide any examples of when they were hurt or disappointed by something you said or did in the past? Ask them for advice on what you can do to change your actions in the future. (Do not defend yourself or your prior behavior. Listen, do not interrupt, and remember to thank them for their candor.)

- Ask your coworker what specific behavior change in you would make them feel more comfortable and be more effective in *their* work.

- Be sure to manage the time so that you have ample opportunity to ask your coworker for their recommendations on one behavior to start, one to stop, and one to continue.

(*continued*)

Suggested Questions to Ask Coworkers (*continued*)

When they describe one behavior to start, ask them if they can provide you with an example of when you demonstrated that behavior exceptionally well in the past, so that if you could replicate that behavior in the future in exactly that way, you'd be successful. It is easier to replicate behavior that you have already demonstrated than to create new behaviors.

- Clearly this type of discussion demands a careful examination of deficits and shortcomings. However, you need to be careful not to get stuck in an extended discussion that focuses only on deficits and does not also offer solutions. Be prepared to steer the conversation toward exploring ways to improve your performance by asking your coworker for suggestions on how you can do things better.

It may take you a week or two to schedule discussion times that are convenient for your coworkers. It's worth the wait. They may confirm your own impressions about your strengths and weaknesses or they may provide you with new and important insights about your behavior that you would not have otherwise known. Either way, knowing how your coworkers perceive your behavioral assets and liabilities will help you more accurately target behaviors to start, stop, and continue in order to become more effective at work.

Verbal and Nonverbal Communication Tips

Your ability to ask questions effectively is related to your other communication skills. For example, if you do not listen well to others, you will miss the content of what they are saying, perhaps critical information, and you will also miss essential nonverbal cues. Verbal and nonverbal information is important for knowing what questions to ask and how to ask them. It is crucial to understand as fully as possible what your coworker is thinking and feeling in order to ask the most useful follow-up questions. Tuning into the

(*continued*)

Verbal and Non-Verbal Communication Tips (*continued*)

verbal and nonverbal messages being sent to you not only helps you understand what your coworker is communicating to you but also shows them that you value what they have to say. Other tips:

- Orient your body toward the other person and look at them to communicate nonverbally that they have your full attention and focus. Research on communication reveals that communication is 55 percent nonverbal, 38 percent inflection and tone, and only 7 percent words.[1] So be sure to send nonverbal, "I am listening" messages: keep your arms unfolded and your posture open, make eye contact, lean in toward the other person.

- Practice interactive listening with your coworker. Rather than immediately replying to what the other person has said, offer a summary of what you think you heard. This will increase the accuracy of your listening skills, help you develop empathy and patience, and provide you with opportunities to further discuss important information and concerns.

- Listen to and absorb opposing views. If your coworker says something you disagree with, let them finish what they are saying, try to restate their key points, and ask them to clarify anything that is not clear to you. Restate the points you agree with and explain why you think they are legitimate. Avoid absolutely asking any questions or making remarks while the other person is speaking.

- Let the other person know that you understand and have heard clearly what their concerns and feelings are. Communicate that you respect their feelings and see them as legitimate by saying something like, "It seems that you feel pretty angry about that," "That must have pleased you," "It sounds to me like you are very frustrated."

- There is truth in the claim that you are not learning anything new while you're talking.

- Be sure you tell your coworker that you appreciate their taking their valuable time to provide you with their observations and feedback. It is nice to say this at the start of the conversation and when you finish.

Congratulations!

This brings to a close the part of this book that has been most demanding of your time and attention as you evaluated the data you collected and then wrote responses to many questions. All your work will be consolidated in the next chapter into a brief, easy-to-remember action plan that will serve to guide your change effort. Though you will be concentrating on changing only a few behaviors, these will be high-impact behaviors that you have thought through and know are important for increasing your performance and satisfaction on the job.

Notes

1.   A. Merhabian, "The Inference of Attitudes from the Posture, Orientation, and Distance of a Communicator," *Journal of Consulting Psychology,* 32 (1968): 296–308.

c . h . a . p . t . e . r 8

CHOOSING BEHAVIOR FOR SUCCESS

C ongratulations on having completed so much hard work in the last chapter. If you have already taken the initiative to meet with your coworkers for their input on your behavior at work, you are ready to create your action plan for change, which is the focus of this chapter. If you have not yet had your discussions with your coworkers, you can read this chapter, familiarize yourself with the structure of the action plan, and then meet with coworkers. But I urge you not to skip the discussion with coworkers, who are in a good position to observe and comment on your personality at work.

> *Things may come to those who wait, but only the things left by those who hustle.*
> — Abraham Lincoln

The action plan is a critical tool that provides you with the structure that can help you guide and implement change. The goal of your action plan is simple and clear: to define a set of behaviors to start, stop, and continue that will increase your success and satisfaction at work. You will select just one behavior to start, one to stop, and one to continue. Having a limited agenda for change increases your odds of successfully implementing your plan and will provide a foundation of success to build upon. Many people fall into the trap of trying to change too many things at once. Often these people become overwhelmed by these multiple demands, fail to successfully implement their change agenda, and end up feeling negative and anxious about change. So begin with one behavior to start, one to stop, and one to continue. When you have made sufficient progress with your action plan and are ready to master other behaviors, move on to a new or modified set of behaviors to start, stop, and continue.

If you are unsure of which behaviors to include in your action plan — perhaps because there are several attractive options — select the behaviors that your coworkers perceive as the most important for you to change to increase your effectiveness on the job.

There are two rules to follow when creating your action plan:

1. You must be absolutely clear and specific in identifying the behaviors that you will start, stop, and continue.

2. The behaviors that you choose to start and stop must be interrelated: they must build upon and reinforce one another. The continue component of your action plan can be independent from the start and stop components because to continue a behavior does not require change, simply a conscious effort to continue leveraging an existing strength.

An example of start and stop behaviors that are interrelated comes from my own action plan. My ACT Self-Profile is the Assertive type (see appendix A), and the interrelated behaviors in my action plan were to start listening to others more carefully and to stop interrupting others. The start and stop components in my action plan are mutually reinforcing. By not interrupting others I am forced to listen to them; when I listen to others and completely focus on trying to understand what they are saying, I do not interrupt.

In contrast, an action plan that includes the two behaviors to start — demonstrating more initiative at work and to stop interrupting others — is an example of one in which the start and stop components are not interrelated and not mutually reinforcing. Although an individual's ACT Self-Profile might indicate that these two behavior changes would be helpful, they are unrelated behaviors, do not complement and integrate with each other, and therefore create two distinct developmental agendas. It's difficult enough to implement an action plan where the start and stop components are interrelated, and much more difficult to implement one where the start and stop components do not reinforce each other. Your goal is to design a plan that you will remember, that you can easily articulate, and most important, *that you can and will implement.*

Mike provides an example of an action plan that has well-integrated start and stop behaviors. Mike wanted to take more responsibility for his productivity at work by becoming more results oriented. His ready, aim, aim, aim, shoot work style was creating problems for him on the job. He was not timely in producing results because he spent too much time preparing to work rather than initiating it and addressing details as they arose. Mike's action plan required that he start taking much more initiative in starting projects and stop worrying about getting every detail precisely defined before beginning the work. Mike's natural attention to detail and his depth of experience limit the chances that he'll overlook key details even without his usual extensive planning. Initiating his work sooner helped Mike raise his productivity without a loss of quality.

Sounds great, you say, but how do I actually implement a change in my behavior? Read on.

Think Before You Act

Luckily we humans have the unique ability to think before acting. Though we take great pride in this ability, it is seldom used. To successfully implement a behavior change, you must put this often-dormant ability to work. You must move from being "at effect" of your personality attributes and acting out of habit to being "at cause" of your work behaviors and acting thoughtfully. Being at effect of your personality means to act and react to events out of habit and without thoughtfully considering the implications of your behavior before you act. Acting from habit is not behavior that you consciously choose to show, it is simply behavior that your personality has predisposed you to demonstrate in the past and that you will continue to show in the future until you take active control of your behavior. At the point that you choose to take control of your behavior, you are at cause: you consciously choose particular behaviors to demonstrate rather than behaving from habit. This is the essence of thinking before you act. To think before you act is not magic; it is preparation, commitment, and self-discipline. And with this preparation, commitment, and self-discipline, changing your work behavior becomes a matter of simply *choosing* to behave more effectively and then doing so.

> The mind stretched to a new idea never goes back to its original dimensions.
> — Oliver Wendell Holmes

Your strong and serious commitment to think before you act will provide you with the only tools required to successfully implement your action plan. You must commit yourself to harnessing all your powers of self-discipline, your sense of personal accountability — responsibility and response-ability. Simply by making the effort to think before you act, you move closer to accomplishing your goals. To think before you act is simultaneously a means and an end in your action plan.

Acknowledging a Need to Change

In the previous chapter I stated that a key to successfully implementing behavior change is to view your need for change in a positive rather than punitive way. This important point bears repeating: *acknowledging a need to change and improve is not an indictment of your character; it is a* sign *of character.* Remember this as you create and implement your action plan. Remember also that your action plan and your change efforts are not directed at changing your core personality but at more consciously orchestrating your behavior to make you more effective and satisfied in your current work situation. To be successful in your efforts, you will want to cultivate your abilities to self-monitor your attitudes, feelings, and thoughts — cultivate your "observing ego." As explained in chapter 1, when you enhance your self-monitoring skills embedded in your observing ego, you can use these skills to think before you act and to guide your expression of constructive rather than destructive behavior. Not only has research shown that it has been done before, but also you are about to prove that it can be done again.

The Action Plan

Your first activity in developing an action plan is to look at, study, and get a feel for the action plan worksheet and how it integrates all the information you have compiled to this point. You have devoted considerable thought to your personality and behavior, your work situation, and the person you would like to be. The action plan frames your newly accumulated knowledge and insight and will help you achieve your goals — convert your thoughts into action. The action plan worksheet appears on page 138, and I

> *Our plans miscarry because they have no aim. When a man does not know what harbor he is making for, no wind is the right wind.*
>
> — Seneca

suggest you take a few moments now to familiarize yourself with it. Study the worksheet in the context of what you have learned and then decide if there is anything about you or your work situation that you need to learn more about before you can confidently complete your action plan.

Take Time to Observe

You will find it beneficial to take five to ten days to experiment at work with the ideas and behaviors that are candidates for incorporation into your action plan. These few days will allow you time to test out new behaviors on the job — rather than just thinking about them — and this will provide you with valuable information you will use to increase your odds of successfully implementing your action plan. These days of observation allow you to see your work situation in light of what you have learned about who you are and who you want to be, and just as important, taking five to ten days forces you to think before you act in creating your action plan.

Here are five activities to do over these five to ten days of observation:

1. Become a cultural anthropologist: look at your corporate culture, office politics, and the ways that things get done on your team and in your organization. Then play with ideas of how to develop an action plan that integrates well into your particular work environment. Here are some suggestions for what to look for:

   • Pay special attention to those people who are very effective in your work environment. Perhaps they have great relationship skills, are unusually efficient and productive, display exceptional client-service skills, or appear tremendously satisfied in their work. What behaviors do they show that can serve as a good model for you?

- Watch how people interact around the office and in meetings. Do things get accomplished through formal or informal networks and relationships? What kinds of behaviors help build productive relationships and which behaviors undermine relationships and are considered problematic in your workplace? How do these different behaviors compare and contrast with the behaviors you've displayed in the past and those you are considering for the future?

- What types of situations, activities, and events create stress in the work environment — not just in you but in the social system in general? How do other people show they are stressed? How do coworkers help each other deal with stress? Which people appear to handle stress exceptionally well and which individuals do not? What can you learn from others about how you can manage your own stress more effectively and how you can work with others who are stressed at work?

- What kinds of behaviors are appreciated, respected, and reinforced on your work team and in your organization? Is it appreciated when team members circulate noteworthy articles or reports that relate to the business? Do some people show generosity in bringing pastries or bagels to share with others? How much time do people spend informally but productively chatting about work and nonwork matters? What do people like to laugh about that makes the workday more fun and interesting? What can you learn from your observations?

2. Experiment with new attitudes, ideas, and behaviors on the job to see how others respond. Depending on your assessment results and your development agenda, the attitudes and behaviors you will want to experiment with will vary. But no matter what new attitudes and behaviors make sense for you, new behaviors require practice and fine-tuning. Be on the lookout for good situations to test out new behaviors and be prepared to take advantage of these opportunities as they arise — in or out of your place of work.

- Make a list of the new attitudes and behaviors you want to test out at work. Before each day of work, read your list and check your schedule for any activities that will offer a good opportunity to test a new behavior. Prepare yourself in advance so you are ready to try your new behavior, then use your preparations to guide your behavior in the situation. Literally check off the behaviors on your list as you try them out and then as you approach the end of the days of observation, review your list to be sure you've tested all the important new ideas and behaviors.

- These days of observation offer the perfect opportunity for practice and to collect internal feedback from yourself to see how these new behaviors feel for you and to observe how others respond to your efforts. Pay extra attention to the responses that these new behaviors stimulate in you and in others.

3. Discuss your behavioral work styles and your plans for self-development with friends or family members who can provide you with observations and suggestions to help you be successful in your change effort. Keep an open mind and pay special attention

to practicing your listening skills. Write down their suggestions to be sure that you do not forget them.

4. Talk with peers and coworkers from whom you solicited input and keep the conversation focused on your self-development ideas. You may also want to approach coworkers with whom you've not already talked. You can expect that a vast majority of your coworkers will be delighted to assist you, and keeping others in the loop has a number of advantages:

- It sends a message to those you work with that you value their input and feedback.
- It conveys to others that you are working to improve yourself in your relationships with them.
- It creates some peer pressure for you to walk your talk.
- Finally, while your friends will be delighted to assist and support your self-development, any coworkers whom you may have alienated with past behavior may become supporters of your effort.

5. Describe the behaviors you want to start, stop, and continue with coworkers and friends. Ask them to describe when they saw you demonstrating especially well the behaviors you want to start — so that if you can simply replicate those exact behaviors, you will be successful in your action plan. Ask them questions to help clarify your exact actions so that you fully understand how others perceive your behavior when you excel. Test some of these behaviors on the job during these observation days.

Completing Your Action Plan

After five to ten days of observation, you will have tried out some new behaviors, seen how you and others respond to your new behaviors, and collected plenty of other helpful information about successful behaviors in your place of work. At that point you will be ready and able to complete your action plan.

As an example of the simplicity of an action plan, below are the three behaviors outlined in the action plan that I designed for myself:

- *Start* listening to others and demonstrate all the patience that is required to listen to others completely.
- *Stop* interrupting others. Under no conditions am I to interrupt when someone is talking. If I am at all unsure that the person has finished what they intended to say, I will ask them if they are done. Only then will I respond.
- *Continue* setting high performance standards, because that is an asset that has helped me to achieve good results in the past.

The start and stop components of the action plan work well because I've selected an interrelated set of behaviors that are complementary. When I am listening, I cannot interrupt. When I do not allow myself to interrupt others, I am forced to listen, and often hear important and new ideas that I might not have otherwise heard. (The complete version of my action plan and one other example are in appendix A.)

Susan's Action Plan

A medical services firm conducted a comprehensive annual review process of their top thirty managers and hired me to assess each manager's strengths and development needs, interview their coworkers, and meet with each manager to explain their results and to create an action plan for performance improvement. Susan was the vice president of a booming division and her assessment results showed strengths in virtually every area of measurement (a 360-degree

(continued)

Susan's Action Plan (*continued*)

assessment was used). She was unanimously described as smart, confident, tirelessly dedicated to her work, and the best people manager in the company. However, Susan's coworkers were concerned that she was overworked, that "her work is her whole life," and people worried she would burn out like several other talented managers in the organization had.

Susan was pleased with her assessment results but she said she did not feel nearly as confident as she appeared to others. Though she knew it was irrational, she experienced self-doubts and worried about her work being "good enough." Her worries drove her to constantly take on more work and made her reluctant to set reasonable limits on demands for her time. She traveled weekly, worked late into the evening, did catch-up work on weekends, and her personal life suffered. She said she was "always fighting some flu or cold that I catch on airplanes . . . I guess I just feel worn out." She worried that "if I don't do the work, it won't get done . . . and quality care would be at risk." She was surprised and disappointed that her work associates were aware of her high level of stress, as she had been trying to hide it from others. Susan realized that the company and those it served would miss her immense talents if she did not get better control over her life.

She wanted help in learning to say no to the seemingly limitless requests for her time and to begin to work more reasonable hours that would allow her time for her other interests that she'd been neglecting. I asked Susan to come to our next meeting with a few ideas about behaviors to start, stop, and continue in order to achieve these goals.

Susan came to our next meeting with a list of six behaviors to start, nine behaviors to stop, and two behaviors to continue. Her ideas were all good, but when I asked how she felt about the list, she said, "overwhelmed, but I think I need to do all these things." Here was another example of Susan having difficulty saying no and then feeling overwhelmed by taking on too much work. We pared her list to specific, interrelated behaviors to start, stop, and continue. Susan organized her action plan around the following behaviors:

- Start delegating 25 percent of my work to the subordinates who report to me and are capable of doing this work. The

(*continued*)

Susan's Action Plan (*continued*)

delegated work would include travel, meeting management, and recruiting.

- Stop taking on more work when I know it will create unreasonable schedules and stress for me.
- Continue to manage and mentor my subordinates in order to assure their success in taking on the new responsibilities that I will be delegating to them.

After completing her action plan, Susan met with her staff, shared her plan, and received enthusiastic support. Each team member provided Susan with a list of work activities that they would like delegated to them in order to enrich their own professional development and that would ease the burden on Susan. The team suggested that they help Susan set limits around taking on new responsibilities by coaching her on how to say no when unreasonable requests were made on her time. Finally, team members were excited that Susan would be providing them with continued management and mentoring, knowing that they would be learning new skills from one of the organization's best managers.

Measuring Progress

When you implement a change process it is helpful to create not only goals but also methods for measuring your progress toward your goals. The action plan will ask you to define how you will measure your progress in executing your behavior changes, and following are a few suggestions. Set a date in the future — two or three months after you begin implementing your plan is about right — to take stock of your progress. Mark the date in your planner or on a calendar. You may want to measure your progress by simply evaluating your own thoughts and feelings on your efforts. You might find it helpful to list the specific instances where you successfully implemented your new behaviors and note those situations where progress did not occur, and make adjustments as needed. It is helpful to ask those you work with for their impressions of your progress — especially coworkers whom you apprised of your plans for behavior change when you designed your action plan. Ask them to provide examples of where you were successful in showing new, more effective behaviors and examples where your intentions to demonstrate more effective behaviors fell short. Any or all of these methods are valid ways to measure progress and will allow you to learn from your previous efforts and experiences and make modifications in your action plan as needed.

Now it's your turn. The final activity in this chapter is to complete your action plan on the next page. It is purposefully brief to allow you to consolidate all your thinking in an easy-to-access, easy-to-review, one-page format. Make a photocopy — or several — of the blank worksheet so that you can work with it again in the future. Complete your action plan in pencil to allow for ongoing editing and modification.

Action Plan Worksheet for: _____

Date: ___/___/___

The focus of your action plan is new behaviors to start and to stop. These two sets of behaviors must be interrelated and complement each other. The behavior to continue is a strength that you will want to demonstrate even more frequently in the future to improve your performance. See appendix A for two sample action plans that are completed.

Behavior I will START: _____
  • (Explain) _____

Behavior I will STOP: _____
  • (Explain) _____

Behavior I will CONTINUE: _____
  • (Explain) _____

This strength can be shown more frequently in these situations:

My Start and Stop behaviors complement each other:

Benefits to implementing these behavior changes:

In the past I've had difficulties with these behaviors when:

Methods to overcome these difficulties:

I've done these behaviors very successfully:

Behavioral cues and triggers:

Memory aides I will use:

These people are supporting my behavior change effort:

I will measure my progress by:

The key to successfully implementing your action plan and improving your personality at work is to commit yourself to doing all you can to stay conscious of the behaviors you want to start, stop, and continue. Here are a few methods to consider:

- Make copies of your action plan and place them in prominent places: in your daily planner; as a screen saver on your computer; on your mirror; on the handle of your telephone. After a few days you might find that you stop noticing your action plan in a particular place: move it somewhere else where it will grab your attention.

- Schedule a daily ten-minute time slot to review and think about the behaviors that you will start, stop, and continue. Review your action plan and create an implementation plan for each day. You might choose to do this at breakfast, on the bus on the way to work, on your coffee break, or during your lunch break. Don't overestimate the effectiveness of your newfound willpower over the behavior patterns you've spent years developing. And don't underestimate the value of creating methods that will grab your attention and remind you of the behaviors that you know will make you more effective. You are waging a great internal battle that deserves ten minutes of strategic thinking every day!

- Write a few words on a note card or sticky note that captures the essence of your start, stop, and continue behaviors. Place the note on the plastic divider in your daily planner that marks "today," or on your computer monitor or the telephone you use. I created a new stop, start, and continue sticky note each day for months to keep my goals firmly in my sight and mind. I found it incredibly helpful to write my target behavior cues as simply as possible:

- Listen
- Don't Ever Interrupt
- Set High Standards

FIND A PARTNER

Almost anyone can benefit by involving someone whom they trust and respect in their self-development efforts. In a recent survey of thirteen thousand executives at 120 companies, 70 percent of the respondents said coaching was very important for professional development, yet a recent study by McKinsey and Company found that only about 30 percent reported they were getting that coaching.[1] Coaching and feedback are especially important when you undertake a behavior-change program. Schedule a weekly half-hour session with a trusted work associate to discuss your plan, your progress, and the frustrations that are bound to occur. Use the sessions with your associate to think through new ideas, to problem solve, and to get feedback to assist you in the process of change.

- If this trusted associate is your boss, this provides three advantages. First, your boss is in a good position to observe your on-the-job behavior and informally coach and mentor you (something a boss is paid to do anyway, and it is in their own self-interest). Second, sharing your action plan with your boss sends the message that you take your self-development seriously and are committed to improving your work performance. Third, you may find that your boss will work especially hard to support your development efforts in ways that he or she previously had not. The seriousness you show in your efforts to develop can positively influence your boss's behavior.
- If you do not trust your boss (enough) to be your

partner, which is not uncommon, seek out someone else in the organization who is in a position to observe your work behavior, is familiar with the other members of your work group, and understands your roles and responsibilities.

FIND A COACH OR THERAPIST

For some people the information, exercises, action plan and suggestions in the book will be the trigger for real behavior change. Some of you may want or need additional support, to help you save your job, get a promotion, or cope with overwhelming work-related stress. If you can afford it, consider hiring a personal coach or therapist. There are many qualified professionals who have the formalized training and experience and who can help you change your behavior. These professionals may be found through your health insurance, a company employee-assistance program, in a community mental health center, or privately. Many people unnecessarily shy away from any type of psychotherapy because of the stigma associated with mental disorders. But the fact is that psychotherapists are called mental *health* professionals because they provide services for normal, healthy people who want to be even more successful and satisfied in their private and work lives.

MEASURE YOUR PROGRESS AND REWARD IT

An effective way to sustain your change effort is to measure and reward your progress. Personal development advances one step at a time, and each step is real progress. Allow yourself psychological and tangible rewards with each progressive step you take.

Think of a concrete reward for your efforts and your progress at the end of each week, month, or quarter. Because your efforts deserve it, reward yourself. A reward can be a special lunch, a round of golf, tickets to a favorite event, permission to take a mental health day off if you are ahead of schedule, your favorite chocolate — whatever appeals to you as a reward.

Also, reward your spirit and soul for the progress you make. Spend time with people whom you like, who like you, and who can provide you with support and reinforcement. Spend time with people who offer you encouragement and with whom you can share both your progress and your setbacks. Don't underestimate how rewarding it can feel to call an old friend, family member, former colleague, or a teacher from earlier days who will recognize and value your achievements.

Note

1.   Ed Michaels, Helen Handfeld-Jones, and Beth Axelrod, *The War for Talent* (Boston: HBR Press, 2002).

c . h . a . p . t . e . r   9

REGENERATING CHARACTER EVERY DAY

C hanging behavior is hard. I have emphasized that maintaining an optimistic attitude toward your efforts to change your behavior is essential for success. And you have put in considerable work to craft a specific plan that defines which behaviors you will start, stop, and continue and how you will implement that plan. You have anticipated obstacles to your progress and described how you will overcome those impediments. You have been introduced to an array of methods, tools, and memory aides to help you succeed in your change effort. But it would be silly not to acknowledge that change is difficult and will present challenges to you every day. There are, however, ways to successfully meet and learn from these challenges.

For example, paying close attention to those instances where you have been effective in implementing your action plan will help you replicate the exact thoughts and behaviors that brought you success. Remember exactly what you were thinking that led to your successful actions. What was the cue in yourself or in that situation that triggered your effective response? Write the thoughts and cues that work well for you into your action plan, burn them into your memory, and use them in the future to trigger more successful behaviors.

Situations in which you've failed or had difficulty implementing your plan are just as instructive as those where you succeeded. Check to see if you were careful to think before you acted in those particular situations. If you consciously tried to guide your actions and it just didn't work out, discover what went wrong in that situation and make corrections the next time similar circumstances arise. If you did not take care to think before acting in a certain situation, think about what you can do differently the next time to trigger thinking before acting and a successful application of your action plan. Never stop generating new methods to trigger your ability to think before you act. Simple memory aids work: put a rubber band around your wrist, strategically place a small note so it is visible to you, put your watch on upside down — any trigger to start, stop, and continue behaviors is worthwhile. If the situation allows for it, ask the person you are with to remind you to implement the specific behaviors (not criticize, speak your mind, listen up, not interrupt, feel free to say no, et cetera) in your action plan. Train yourself to recognize cues or red flags that offer warning that you are approaching a situation where you might have difficulty implementing a behavior you have identified as important for increased effectiveness and satisfaction. Be alert for those cues or red flags and train yourself to take an extra moment in those situations to think before you act and you will find you are much more effective in your efforts to generate constructive behaviors that reflect the person you want to be.

Example of a Red Flag

For the argumentative individual who seeks to be a better listener, a big red flag is the expression "Yes, but." "Yes, but" is really a disguised "No"; it sounds like agreement but actually focuses on what

(continued)

Example of a Red Flag (*continued*)

is wrong with what someone is saying rather than what value it has. Here's an example: "Jack, I think it would be a good idea if we proofread each other's work to make sure we catch all the errors." "Yes, but I don't have time for that." "Well, you could delegate some of the less-sophisticated work to our support team." "Yes, but I don't trust their work." Such "yes, but" responses show that a person is not listening; they are focused on their own position and on finding fault with someone else's suggestions. For individuals who want to start listening better, simply replacing "yes, but" with "yes, and" can make all the difference: "Jack, I think it would be a good idea if we proofread each other's work to make sure we catch all the errors." "Yes, and I need to find a way to leave myself enough time to do that." "Well, you could delegate some of the less-sophisticated work to our support team." "Yes, and let's find a way to assure the quality of their work." "Good point. I can ask Bob to help out on that; he's good with the support team."

You are far better prepared to manage red-flag situations than before you began this journey of self-discovery and self-improvement. You have constructed a plan that targets very specific behaviors, and you can have confidence that these behavior changes will yield significant personal and professional gains. While your ability to manage your behavior may be severely tested at times by work associates who have less-than-optimal personality styles, remind yourself that you and only you are in control of your attitudes and behavior. Coworkers may create conditions that make it more difficult for you to control your behavior, but they do not control your behavior — only you control your behavior, and that is exactly what you have committed yourself to do. It would be unrealistic to expect that you can effectively direct all your behaviors all the time in all situations; but, in order to realize what you've envisioned for yourself and the goals you've set, it's vital to make a conscious effort to enact changes every day. Each day starts with a clean slate, and you can choose the behaviors you will exhibit and apply toward creating your most effective and satisfying self at work.

And finally, if you find yourself at times thinking your personality is set and can't be changed, remind yourself that your behavior is entirely within your control. The challenges we face at work are complex and sometimes formidable, and many are outside our control. There are in fact very few things you can hope to control; but the one thing you can control — your behavior — changes everything.

ACT SELF-PROFILE

This appendix provides two completed action plans, as described in chapter 8. In that chapter, you were asked to create a personal Action Plan based on the results of your Self-Profile. The action plan is a critical tool that can help you implement change. The goal of the action plan is simple and clear: to define a set of behaviors to start, stop, and continue that will increase your success and satisfaction at work. These two sample action plans — one of which is my own — present an opportunity to see how others have created their Action Plan. My hope is that these sample Action Plans will be useful tools to help you create or modify your own Action Plan.

Completed Sample Action Plan Worksheets

Action Plan Worksheet for: Ronald Warren
Date: 3/22/2001

The focus of your action plan is new behaviors to start and to stop. These two sets of behaviors must be interrelated and complement each other. The behavior to continue is a strength that you will want to demonstrate more frequently to improve your performance.

Behavior I will START: Listening Better
- *This means listening with 100 percent attention focused on what the other person is communicating.*

Behavior I will STOP: Interrupting Others
- *This means NEVER interrupting...when I catch myself, say "excuse me, please go on."*

Behavior I will CONTINUE: Setting High Standards
- *Be very conscientious in maintaining quality; provide our team with detail focus.*

This strength can be shown more frequently in these situations: *Reviewing all final materials before they are printed or sent to customers.*

My Start and Stop behaviors complement each other: *The two go hand-in-hand; listening is exactly what I do while NOT interrupting. If I catch myself interrupting, I need to start listening.*

Benefits to implementing these behavior changes: *Listening attentively better assures I hear information I miss with sloppy listening. Stopping my interrupting will upgrade my social, communication, and teamwork skills, which need improvement.*

In the past I've had difficulties with these behaviors when: *1. I focus on my own thoughts and not on what the other person*

(continued)

Completed Sample Action Plan Worksheets
(continued)

is saying; 2. I get passionate and excited about something and talk rather than listen; 3. In discussions & arguments I focus on "winning" rather than on understanding; 4. I feel rushed and hurried...I get pushy, impatient.

Methods to overcome these difficulties: 1. Read Action Plan each morning before work; 2. Ask friends to let me know if I've interrupted; 3. Rubber band on index finger; 4. Prep before each meeting to remind myself not to interrupt.

I've done these behaviors very successfully: On sales calls, a situation where I am acutely aware of being polite and on my best behavior. When I actively am seeking agreement and make a conscious effort, I am very successful.

Behavioral cues and triggers: THE cue is the sound of someone else talking...if I hear two people talking at once and one of them is me, it will trigger me to stop talking and start listening. Visual cue: rubber band on finger.

Memory aides I will use: Sticky note on bathroom mirror at home; rubber band on index finger at work.

These people are supporting my behavior change effort: My entire work team is aware of my plan. Sandra and Barry have agreed to point their right index finger up to the ceiling to signal me to start listening or not to interrupt.

I will measure my progress by: Daily review of day's success and setbacks each evening on bus ride home from the office. After two months I will collect feedback from the team on successes and shortcomings, asking for explicit examples of each and revising my plan as indicated.

Completed Sample Action Plan Worksheets

Action Plan Worksheet for: M. L. Johnson
Date: 4/6/2002

The focus of your action plan is new behaviors to start and to stop. These two sets of behaviors must be interrelated and complement each other. The behavior to continue is a strength that you will want to demonstrate more frequently to improve your performance.

Behavior I will START: Speaking Up
- *I will speak up more, be assertive, and clearly state my positions and point of view.*

Behavior I will STOP: Agreeing Too Easily
- *I will no longer passively agree to things I disagree with to avoid conflicts with team members.*

Behavior I will CONTINUE: Being Friendly and Warm with My Teammates
- *I will continue to make an extra effort to get to know my teammates and to provide leadership in our informal social network. Others seldom initiate social activities, but most participate and it's good for team morale.*

This strength can be shown more frequently in these situations: *Organizing more team activities (lunches, off-sites, speakers) at team meetings.*

My Start and Stop behaviors complement each other: *I need to speak up in order to stop agreeing to things too easily. In the past I've just sat in silence and have passively agreed to things by not addressing them.*

Benefits to implementing these behavior changes: *I will have greater influence and grow in my position. By not agreeing too easily, I will avoid assignments I do not want and ensure more assignments to projects I want to work on.*

(*continued*)

Completed Sample Action Plan Worksheets
(continued)

In the past I've had difficulties with these behaviors when: *I get intimidated by more vocal and pushy people. It is hard to get the floor, to say what I think. I give up too easily.*

Methods to overcome these difficulties: *If there is too much commotion to get noticed, I will literally raise my hand. That seems to silence others and enables me to get the floor. I will be prepared by practicing expressing my wants with Jill prior to the meetings.*

I've done these behaviors very successfully: *When I am the acknowledged expert on the topic, I am more comfortable speaking up and holding my ground. Part of being expert is being prepared, which I will be, on topics that I need to be more assertive about.*

Behavioral cues and triggers: *I usually feel nervous. I can feel it in my gut. I will think of that nervousness as a trigger... as energy I can use to fuel my assertiveness. A visual cue is the sticky note I've put in my planner that I look at constantly; it says, SPEAK UP!*

Memory aides I will use: *Sticky note I've put in my planner. Jill said she will ask me, "M. L., how's that for you?"*

These people are supporting my behavior change effort: *My team enthusiastically endorses my goals. Jill is my communications coach; Brian and my manager, Carla, have agreed to ask me to speak up more often.*

I will measure my progress by: *Creating a checklist of the top five issues/projects that will be discussed in meetings during the week and rate how assertive (1= not assertive; 5 = very assertive) I was on each. At the end of three months I will do an overall review of my scores with Jill.*

a . p . p . e . n . d . i . x   b

THE PROFILE TYPE LIBRARY

This Profile Type Library describes twenty-two common ACT Profile Types. Each ACT Profile Type is made up of a combination of three to six of the highest scores in an ACT Profile. For example, high scores on Scales 3, 4, 5 make up the Cautious Type; high scores on Scales 1, 2, 3, 4 make up the Social Type; high scores on Scales 6, 7, 8, 9, 10, 11 form the Forceful Driven Type. In the pages that follow, a brief description of the most prominent behaviors is provided for each Profile Type.

Determining Your Profile Type

If you completed the ACT assessment online, you have received a short description of your Profile Type or you may have purchased your ACT Self-Profile Report that includes an in-depth description of your Profile Type, item and scale scores, and recommendations for improvement. If you have not completed an online assessment and would like to get your own ACT Profile Report, please visit: www.psychtests.com/act/

If you completed your self-assessment and plotted your ACT Self-Profile manually in chapter 2, you can determine your Profile Type by finding the one in the Profile Type Library that most closely matches the highest scores in your ACT Self-Profile. Here are a few considerations in selecting a good match:

You may find more than one Profile Type that is a good match to your ACT Self-Profile. If that is the case, study the types that are a good match for you and learn from each one.

If Scale 5 — Tense — is one of your highest scores: for the moment, put aside your Tense Scale and find the best matches using your next highest scores. For example, if your highest scores are on Scales 1, 2, and 5 (or 3, 4, 5; or 5, 6, 7; or 5, 8, 9; or 5, 10, 11), find the next-highest scores that are prominent in your profile. Then find the Profile Type in the Library that matches these scores. It is important for you to understand what other personality traits are playing a prominent role in driving your behavior besides tension and apprehension.

If eight or more of your ACT scale scores are greater than 70 percent: you match the Expanded Profile Type. About 5 percent of people have expanded profiles and these individuals tend to behave like their profiles: expansive, changeable, expressive, complex.

If none of your scores are above 25 percent: you match the Constricted Profile Type. This is relatively rare and people with a constricted profile are like their profiles: cautious, guarded, and judgmental.

Profile Type Library

1. The Social Type: Scales 1, 2, 3, 4 are prominent
2. The Feeling Type: Scales 1, 2, 5 are prominent
3. The Moody Type: Scales 1, 2, 6, 7 are prominent
4. The Motivated Type: Scales 1, 2, 8, 9 are prominent
5. The Balanced Type: Scales 1, 2, 10, 11 are prominent
6. The Balanced-Deferring Type: Scales 1, 2, 3, 4, 10, 11 are prominent
7. The Balanced-Tense Type: Scales 1, 2, 5, 10, 11 are prominent
8. The Balanced-Aggressive Type: Scales 1, 2, 6, 7, 10, 11 are prominent
9. The Balanced-Competitive Type: Scales 1, 2, 8, 9, 10, 11 are prominent
10. The Cautious Type: Scales 3, 4, 5 are prominent
11. The Conflicted Type: Scales 3, 4, 6, 7 are prominent
12. The Bureaucratic Type: Scales 3, 4, 8, 9 are prominent
13. The Reliable Type: Scales 3, 4, 10, 11 are prominent
14. The "Type A": Scales 5, 6, 7 are prominent
15. The Intense Type: Scales 5, 8, 9 are prominent
16. The Ambivalent Type: Scales 5, 10, 11 are prominent
17. The Aggressive Type: Scales 6, 7, 8, 9 are prominent
18. The Assertive Type: Scales 6, 7, 10, 11 are prominent
19. The Driven Type: Scales 8, 9, 10, 11 are prominent
20. The Forceful Driven Type: Scales 6, 7, 8, 9, 10, 11 are prominent
21. The Expanded Type: more than eight Scales are prominent
22. The Constricted Type: less than three Scales are prominent

The Profile Types

The Social Type
(highest scores on Scales 1, 2, 3, 4)

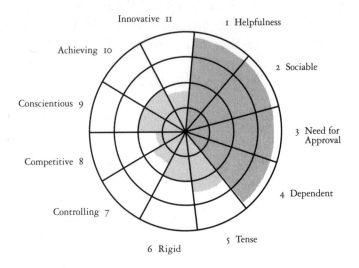

- Prefers to follow the lead of others
- Easygoing, defers to others; not pushy or aggressive
- Low results-orientation; low initiative
- Team player; cooperates with ease
- Socially outgoing and friendly
- Supportive and encouraging
- Patient, good listener
- Kind, considerate, careful not to offend others
- Trusting, generous, very forgiving of others
- Avoids risk; conservative, conventional and conforming
- Talkative; sometimes assertive, but never forceful

The Feeling Type
(highest scores on Scales 1, 2, 5)

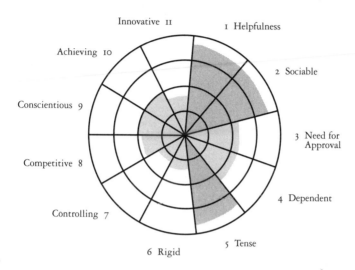

Innovative 11   1 Helpfulness

Achieving 10

2 Sociable

Conscientious 9

3 Need for Approval

Competitive 8

4 Dependent

Controlling 7

6 Rigid   5 Tense

- Sociable; friendly; likes people
- Considerate of others; kind-hearted
- Tentative; insecure; low self-confidence
- May be reserved or restrained in groups
- Self-doubting; insecure
- Nervous; anxious
- Supportive and encouraging of others, hard on self
- Cooperative, works well in groups
- Prefers to avoid conflict; dislikes confrontation and disagreements

The Moody Type
(highest scores on Scales 1, 2, 6, 7)

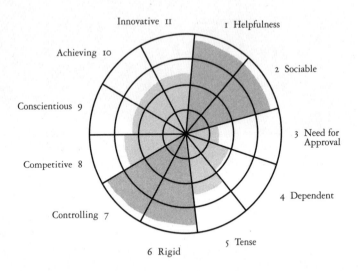

- Likes to be the one in control; wants to do things his/her way
- Wants to lead
- Moody
- Sarcastic and cynical
- Impulsive
- Passionate about friendships, values, beliefs
- Friendly, but combative; socially inconsistent
- Likes people, but does not fully trust them
- Seeks excitement, stimulation, activity; gets bored easily
- Very assertive, expressive, opinionated
- Gets upset and angry easily; quick temper; argumentative
- Strong sense of urgency; in a hurry

Unusual combination of traits — very possibly will be perceived by others as aggressive and rigid and far less patient and sociable.

The Motivated Type
(highest scores on Scales 1, 2, 8, 9)

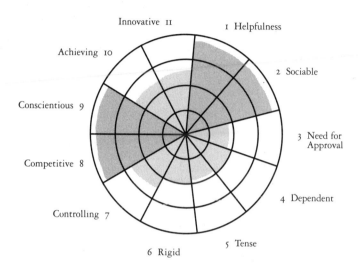

Innovative 11
1 Helpfulness
Achieving 10
2 Sociable
Conscientious 9
3 Need for Approval
Competitive 8
4 Dependent
Controlling 7
5 Tense
6 Rigid

- Assertive; good at expressing thoughts and feelings
- Strong work ethic; believes in working hard
- Determined and persistent
- Ambitious; highly motivated to be successful
- Spontaneous and fun-loving
- Enjoys working with others, cooperative
- Good listening skills; takes others' ideas and suggestions seriously
- Energetic; enthusiastic; very expressive
- Concern for quality and timeliness
- Persuasive, but not pushy
- A natural salesperson

The Balanced Type
(highest scores on Scales 1, 2, 10, 11)

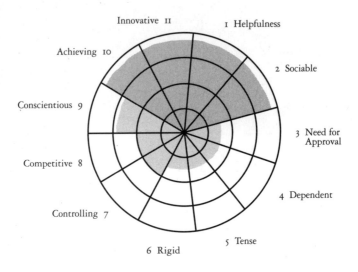

- Confident; relaxed; secure
- Optimistic
- Enjoys hard work and enjoys people
- Thoughtful; considerate; kind
- Takes the initiative
- Likes challenging work
- Strong leadership skills
- Patient; willing to take time with others
- Likes teams and believes in teamwork
- Flexible and open-minded
- A good listener; seeks out others' input and feedback
- Interpersonally skilled
- Interested in self-development and in the development of others

The Balanced-Deferring Type
(highest scores on Scales 1, 2, 3, 4, 10, 11)

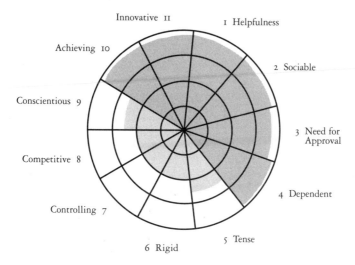

- Confident, yet modest
- Ambitious; wants to succeed
- Willing to lead or defer to the lead of others
- Sets high standards; disciplined; strong work ethic
- Conscientious and detail-oriented
- Enjoys challenging tasks
- Enjoys people and projects
- Very patient and available; willing to take time with others
- Supportive and encouraging
- Cooperative; likes teamwork
- Flexible and open-minded, always ready to hear another opinion
- A good listener; seeks out others' input and feedback
- Enjoys socializing and being with people
- Quietly assertive; never aggressive or pushy
- Interested in self-development and in developing others

The Balanced-Tense Type
(highest scores on Scales 1, 2, 5, 10, 11)

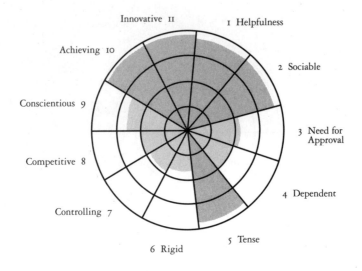

- Generally confident and secure; has underlying insecurities and bouts of self-doubt and worry
- Enjoys challenging tasks
- Has lots of energy, some of it nervous energy
- Ambitious; wants to be successful
- Creative; full of good ideas
- Flexible and open-minded
- High initiative; good follow-through
- Patient; willing to take time with others
- Likes teams and teamwork
- Enjoys the company of others; socially skilled; respectful
- Good listener
- Assertive

The Balanced-Aggressive Type
(highest scores on Scales 1, 2, 6, 7, 10, 11)

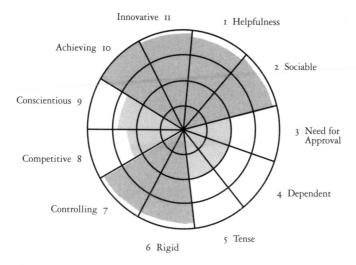

Innovative 11   1 Helpfulness

Achieving 10

Conscientious 9

Competitive 8

Controlling 7

2 Sociable

3 Need for Approval

4 Dependent

6 Rigid   5 Tense

- Confident; assertive; can get cocky
- Likes to be in charge; wants to be the leader
- Very high initiative; driven and intense
- Enthusiastic and passionate
- Fun; spontaneous; energetic
- Often composed and calm but has a quick temper and gets angry
- Has an abundance of good ideas and the drive to act on these ideas
- Thinks of self as relatively patient, but subject to impatience, hurry, sense of urgency
- Likes teams and teamwork but can get combative and adversarial
- Socially skilled: clever, charming, can be entertaining
- Outwardly flexible and open-minded, but becomes stubborn and inflexible
- Sees self as calm, patient, social, and willing to listen; may be seen by others as more high-strung and pushy, less patient and sociable

The Balanced Competitive Type
(highest scores on Scales 1, 2, 8, 9, 10, 11)

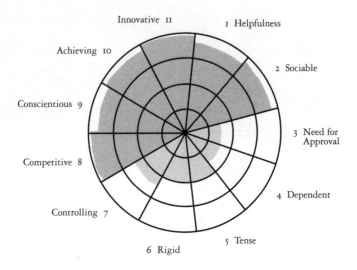

- A natural salesperson: persuasive, ambitious, hard-working, and likes to help others
- Confident; secure; comfortable with self and others
- Driven to succeed
- Competitive; wants to be a winner, the best
- Has initiative and self-direction
- Fun; spontaneous; energetic
- Patient and supportive of others
- Likes teams and teamwork
- Flexible and open-minded; creative and inquisitive
- Good listener; seeks out others' input and feedback
- Able to derive pleasure from challenging tasks and from socializing
- Works well independently or on a team
- Won't miss many details; very conscientious; does due diligence
- Likes to lead; wants to be in a position of influence, responsibility

The Cautious Type
(highest scores on Scales 3, 4, 5)

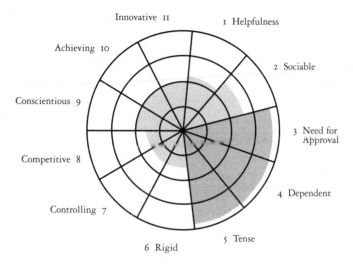

Innovative 11   1 Helpfulness
Achieving 10   2 Sociable
Conscientious 9
Competitive 8   3 Need for Approval
Controlling 7   4 Dependent
6 Rigid   5 Tense

- Reliable
- Generous to others
- Conservative; avoids risks
- Low-key; reserved and cautious
- Low initiative; limited ambition and drive
- Cooperative; does not want to "make waves"
- Conforming and conventional
- Avoids conflict and controversy
- Pessimistic; low self-confidence
- Works best with gentle support in a well-structured workplace
- Anxious and tense
- Not assertive
- Over-accommodating to others

See Deferring Sector in chapter 3 on this combination of traits.

The Conflicted Type
(highest scores on Scales 3, 4, 6, 7)

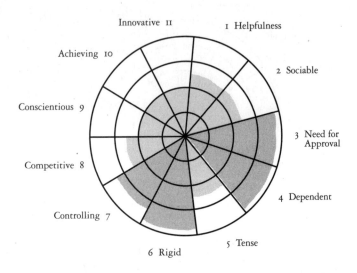

- Inconsistent behavior: can be deferential at one moment and aggressive the next
- Has very strong beliefs
- Conservative
- Prefers routine; likes structure and rules
- Moody; gets angry and irritable
- Finds it difficult to relax, enjoy things
- May behave impulsively
- Rigid; tends to be quietly stubborn
- Works best in a structured, low-stress workplace
- Experiences anxiety and worry

The Bureaucratic Type
(highest scores on Scales 3, 4, 8, 9)

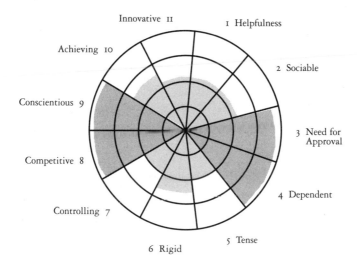

- Motivated to produce high-quality results
- Wants to get along with others
- Serious; not often spontaneous
- Disciplined; detail-oriented
- Can work well independently or on a team
- Likes to be noticed and recognized for efforts
- Analytical; prefers to look carefully before leaping
- A perfectionist; may not produce timely results
- Conservative
- Respectful to others; diplomatic
- Reliable and restrained; not impulsive
- Likes rules and procedures
- Works best in a structured setting
- Motivated to get along with others

The Reliable Type
(highest scores on Scales 3, 4, 10, 11)

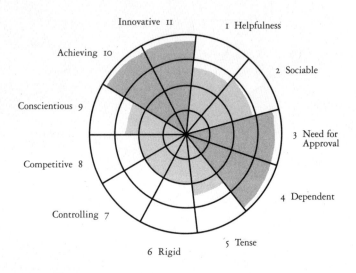

- Reticent leader; prefers not to be in the limelight
- Willing to try new things but respects the tried-and-true
- Organized and disciplined
- Motivated to succeed, to do good work
- Enjoys challenges
- Sets high standards
- Detail-oriented; precise
- Modest and unassuming
- Respectful and considerate toward others; diplomatic
- Believes in teamwork; likes to help others
- Willing to compromise with others
- Good listener
- Sometimes confident, sometimes tentative

The "Type A"
(highest scores on Scales 5, 6, 7)

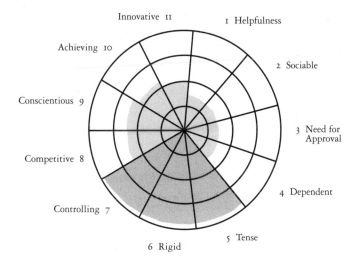

- Gets angry easily; temperamental; experiences lots of hostility
- Tends to be critical and demanding of others
- Driven and aggressive
- Agitated; lots of nervous energy
- Controlling; likes to do things his/her way
- Tough-minded; not very sympathetic to others
- Self-absorbed; concerned with own needs and wants
- Hurried; impatient; high sense of urgency
- Prefers to talk rather than listen
- Not particularly cooperative; not a team player
- Anxious when uncertain
- Worries about what is wrong, could go wrong, may not be right
- Has an impulsive streak; rebellious
- Opinionated; stubborn
- Very assertive, pushy, forceful

The Intense Type
(highest scores on Scales 5, 8, 9)

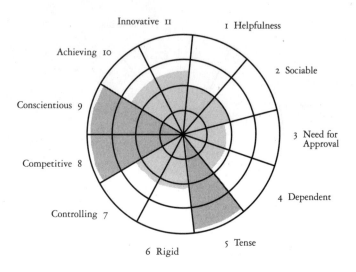

- A perfectionist; has very high performance standards
- Focused on projects and tasks, not people
- Assertive; persuasive; values competence and being right
- Very competitive; wants to be seen as a winner and is insecure about losing
- Wants to be in a position of influence and responsibility
- Wants to make an impact that is visible
- Driven to succeed; persistent; hard-working
- Detail-oriented
- Self-absorbed
- Prefers to talk rather than listen
- High energy; passionate
- Nervous; tense; worries about what is wrong, can go wrong, may not be right
- Very serious, has difficulty relaxing; needs to stop and smell the roses

The Ambivalent Type
(highest scores on Scales 5, 10, 11)

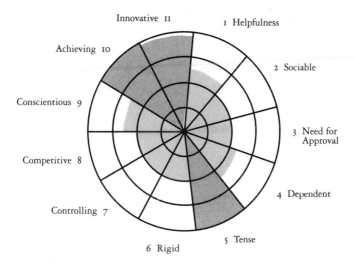

- Ambitious
- Ambivalent: varies between confident and insecure
- Seeks out challenging projects and tasks, but feels stressed by too much challenge
- Likes to be creative, innovate
- Has a lot of energy, some nervous energy
- Unconventional; non-conforming
- Sets high standards
- Driven and determined to succeed
- Confident, but not optimistic
- Likes to think; likes to find and solve problems
- Anxious and tense
- Moody

The Aggressive Type
(highest scores on Scales 6, 7, 8, 9)

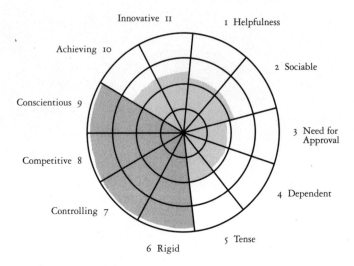

- Results-oriented
- Believes in hard work; driven to succeed
- Likes to play devil's advocate
- Assertive and passionately persuasive
- Independent and rebellious
- Controlling; forceful; pushy
- Demanding; a perfectionist
- Quick-tempered; abrupt; argumentative; impatient
- Takes a no-nonsense approach to work; takes no prisoners
- Self-absorbed; a poor listener; resists input from others
- Not particularly cooperative; not a team player
- Sarcastic; may say or do things that hurt others' feelings
- A strong sense of urgency; is hurried, harried, hassled
- Opinionated and inflexible: sees issues as black and white, little room for gray
- Fault-finding; may focus more on problems than solutions

See Domineering Sector in chapter 3 on this combination of traits.

The Assertive Type
(highest scores on Scales 6, 7, 10, 11)

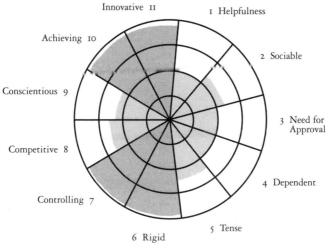

Innovative 11   1 Helpfulness

Achieving 10   2 Sociable

Conscientious 9

3 Need for
Approval

Competitive 8

4 Dependent

Controlling 7

6 Rigid   5 Tense

- Ambitious
- Wants to be in charge; likes to have and wield influence
- Very decisive
- A risk-taker; likes excitement
- Enjoys challenging projects and tasks
- Likes to be creative, innovate
- Enthusiastic; energetic; a fervent believer and promoter
- Unconventional; non-conforming; rebellious
- Sets high standards; persistent and determined
- Confident, but not an optimist
- Likes to think; likes to find and solve problems; likes to learn
- Focused on own needs, interests, and projects; not focused on other people
- Not particularly cooperative; not a team player
- Not suggestible, naive, or easily influenced
- Likes to laugh; clever; can be quick-witted
- In a hurry; hates to waste time; has a high sense of urgency
- Has difficulty listening, getting input from others
- Very assertive; can be argumentative, adversarial

The Driven Type
(highest scores on Scales 8, 9, 10, 11)

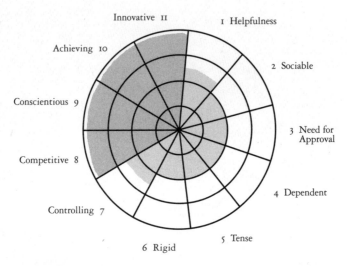

- Confident and optimistic
- Very assertive
- Decisive; willing to take calculated risks
- Very strong work ethic; enjoys work
- Sets high performance standards; sometimes standards are unrealistic
- Energetic, enthusiastic, and entertaining; likes to have fun
- Believes in persuasion; inspired about a point of view; considers it important to be competent and right
- Competitive; a person who likes to be seen as a winner; relishes being the best
- Independent thinker; non-conforming
- Creative and innovative; likes to find clever solutions to problems
- Likes to lead; wants a position of influence, responsibility; wants to have an impact
- Able to get along with others when motivated to do so
- Focused more on projects and tasks than people and feelings
- Needs stimulation and activity; easily bored by routine, mundane tasks

The Forceful Driven Type
(Highest scores on Scales 6, 7, 8, 9, 10, 11)

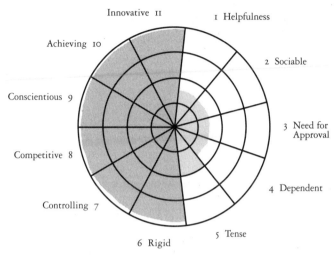

- Confident; cocky
- Alternately optimistic and pessimistic
- Independent thinker; non-conforming
- Likes risks; very decisive; impulsive
- Persuasive, passionate, and inspired
- Creative and innovative; likes to find clever solutions to problems
- Likes to lead; wants to influence and have responsibility
- Enjoys challenges; has a strong work ethic
- Sets high, sometimes unrealistic, performance standards
- Can get pushy, forceful, impatient
- Self-absorbed
- Will listen to others when motivated to do so; generally prefers to talk
- Needs stimulation; bored by routine
- Energetic, enthusiastic, and entertaining; likes to be the center of attention
- May have difficulty being a team player

The Expanded Type

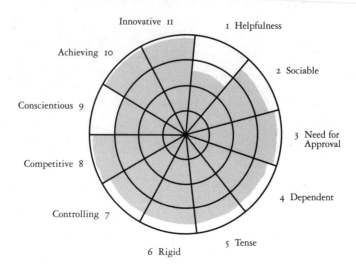

- A "live wire"
- Energetic; enthusiastic; passionate
- Labile; capricious; changeable; moody; ambivalent
- Inquisitive; interested in many things
- Full of ideas; tends to be undisciplined
- Friendly, outgoing, and sociable; loves being with people
- Cares about others, always willing to "lend an ear"
- Wants to be liked by others
- Emotional and intense
- Opinionated but open-minded; has an opinion, but is willing to listen to others
- Thrives on stimulation; likes exciting things
- Upset by conflict
- Expressive, animated, if not flamboyant
- Sometimes all over the place, like their ACT Profile

The Constricted Type

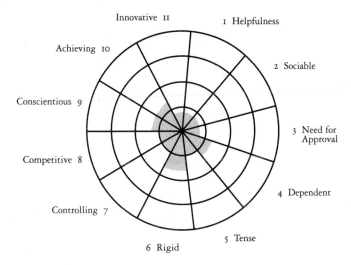

- Conscientious and hardworking
- Reliable
- Formal, conservative; not casual or loose; reserved in attitudes and behavior
- Controlling; tends to be inflexible; does not compromise easily
- Careful; does not like risk; wants to know the facts and the figures
- Strict; serious; not light-hearted
- Suspicious; does not take things at face value
- Expects others to prove their value and worth
- Private; introverted; not interested in meeting people or making small talk
- Tends to keep emotions to self
- Reserved in attitudes and behaviors
- Judgmental: carefully evaluates people and situations before making commitments
- Assertive, but a person of few words

r.e.c.o.m.m.e.n.d.e.d
r.e.a.d.i.n.g

Bardwick, Judith. *Danger in the Comfort Zone.* New York: AMACOM, 1993.

Benson, Herbert. *The Relaxation Response.* New York: Avon Books, 1975.

Gardner, Howard. *Intelligence Reframed.* New York: Basic Books, 1999.

Goleman, Daniel. *Emotional Intelligence.* New York: Bantam Books, 1995.

Hoffman, Edward. *Psychological Testing at Work.* New York: McGraw-Hill, 2002.

Moore, Thomas. *Care of the Soul.* New York: HarperCollins, 1992.

Oldham, John, and Lois Morris. *The Personality Self-Portrait.* New York: Bantam Books, 1990.

Seligman, Martin. *Learned Optimism.* New York: Pocket Books, 1990.

Sternberg, Robert. *Successful Intelligence.* New York: Penguin Books, 1997.

Tannen, Deborah. *Talking from 9 to 5.* New York: William Morrow, 1994.

i . n . d . e . x

I

ignoring one's personality and
   behavior, 97–98
impulsiveness, 41
indecisiveness, 60
independence. *See* Dependent
   scale
Innovative scale, 47–48
insight into one's behavior and
   personality, 8, 97
Intense Type, 174

L

layoffs, 7
leadership skills, 6, 46; self-
   assessment of, x–xi. *See
   also* managers
locus of control: external, 36;
   internal, 46
"loners," 60

M

managers: and Deferential
   sector, 51; gender differences, 48–49; most *vs.* least
   effective, 36, 63–65; nega-
   tive/problematic traits, 54.
   See also boss(es); executives
micromanagers, 45
Mirror Profile, 84, 85; constructing, 86, 112, 115;
   evaluating, 87; self-profile
   compared with, 115–17
Moody Type, 162
Motivated Type, 163
mutli-rater assessments. *See* assessments, 360-degree

N

Need for Approval scale, 33–34
neediness, 43. *See also* Dependent scale
negativity, 37

O

observe, taking time to, 134–37
observing ego, 11, 12, 133
overraters, 90

P

partner, finding a, 144–45
performance, high, 50, 53
personality: importance of, in
   keeping one's job, 7–9; and
   job effectiveness, research
   on, 63–68; nature of, 4–6;
   and work experience, x
personality assessment, 48;
   preemployment, 6–7
personality disorders, 4
personality traits: assessing
   one's, 10–11, 135; counterproductive, 5, 8, 50,
   60–62, 98, 100–101. *See
   also specific topics*
pessimism, 37
problem solving, moving from
   emotions to constructive,
   96–97
procrastinators, 54
professionals, most vs. least effective, 65–66
progress: measuring, 140–41,
   145–46; rewarding, 145–46
purposeful managers, 54

a.c.k.n.o.w.l.e.d.g.m.e.n.t.s

Many people have helped me directly or indirectly on this book and I want to thank them: Mark Brenner, Bil Murray, Dan Cohn, Barry Fishman, Carlton Feronno, Lisa Crespo, Oscar Munoz, George Smith, Lee Sandler, Kathleen Farinacci, David Bennett, Deborah Price, Jeffrey Sonnenfeld, and Eric Bolt.

Thank you, Vivian Garrigues, for your calm and your editing.

Thank you, Kenexa Technologies. Ame Creglow, thanks for working on the assessments with me. Thanks to Roger Lipson for the book title.

At New World Library I was fortunate to work with Georgia Hughes and Katie Farnam Conolly, whose insights, suggestions, and downright demands helped make this a better book.

Thank you, Barry and Rose Warren, Kelly and Will Warren.

Ronald A. Warren, Ph.D., is an organizational psychologist who specializes in employee assessment. Over a million people worldwide have taken assessments Ron has developed: the ACT Profile, MAP11, WorkStyles®, Cockpit 2000, Praxis©, and Praxis IC©.

Ron earned a B.A., *magna cum laude,* in philosophy and psychology from Washington University in St. Louis. He received his M.A. and Ph.D. from the University of Chicago, Committee on Human Development. He has published in *Training Magazine, International Symposium of Aviation Psychology, Measures of Leadership, Adolescence,* and the *American Journal of Psychiatry.* In 1984, Ron cofounded Acumen International, where he was the director of research and development until 1997. Following that, Ron was director of assessment at Kenexa Technologies. Working in the United States and abroad, his clients have included United Parcel Service, Hyatt Hotels, Consumers Union, Walt Disney World

Attractions, British Airways, Maytag, Nippon Manpower, Pella Corporation, DaVita, and Johnson & Johnson.

Ron's firm, achievementparadox.com, provides consulting services to organizations in all areas of organizational measurement, including 360-degree assessments for corporate training programs. achievementparadox.com is based in Novato, California.

The ACT Self-Profile is available free at:
http://www.psychtests.com/act/

MAPii is available at:
achievementparadox.com
and at
pantesting.com

Ron can be e-mailed at ron@achievementparadox.com.

New World Library is dedicated to
publishing books and audios that inspire
and challenge us to improve the quality
of our lives and our world.

Our books and cassettes are available
at bookstores everywhere.
For a complete catalog, contact:

New World Library
14 Pamaron Way
Novato, California 94949

Phone: (415) 884-2100
Fax: (415) 884-2199
Or call toll free: (800) 972-6657
Catalog requests: Ext. 50
Ordering: Ext. 52

E-mail: escort@nwlib.com
newworldlibrary.com